Target your Maths

Year 3-6 Practice Workbook

Answers

Stephen Pearce

Elmwood Education

First published 2018 by
Elmwood Education Limited
Unit 5 Mallow Park
Watchmead
Welwyn Garden City
Herts. AL7 1GX
Tel. 01707 333232

ISBN 9781 906 622 718

Typeset and illustrated by Tech-Set Ltd., Gateshead, Tyne and Wear.

YEAR 3 PRACTICE WORKBOOK ANSWERS

1

1 53	**11** one hundred and sixty
2 200	**12** five hunded and thirty-two
3 731	**13** ninety-seven
4 194	**14** three hundred and fifty-eight
5 961	**15** seven hundred and three
6 512	**16** four hundred and eighty-one
7 640	**17** eight hundred and twenty
8 385	**18** nine hundred and nineteen
9 807	**19** six hundred and five
10 1000	**20** five hundred and seventy-four

2

1 185	**11** 447	**21** 915	**31** 817
2 813	**12** 795	**22** 118	**32** 284
3 656	**13** 258	**23** 752	**33** 525
4 338	**14** 624	**24** 231	**34** 900
5 502	**15** 972	**25** 297	**35** 749
6 250	**16** 319	**26** 660	**36** 351
7 927	**17** 631	**27** 593	**37** 832
8 499	**18** 86	**28** 826	**38** 568
9 771	**19** 197	**29** 449	**39** 196
10 604	**20** 463	**30** 804	**40** 773

3

1 431	**9** 372	**17** 731	**25** 622	**33** 293
2 174	**10** 584	**18** 265	**26** 466	**34** 727
3 323	**11** 863	**19** 203	**27** 193	**35** 902
4 800	**12** 138	**20** 880	**28** 948	**36** 509
5 589	**13** 976	**21** 492	**29** 540	**37** 631
6 227	**14** 638	**22** 908	**30** 312	**38** 256
7 836	**15** 706	**23** 477	**31** 876	**39** 152
8 678	**16** 485	**24** 335	**32** 289	**40** 368

4

1 218	**9** 333	**17** 531	**25** 839	**33** 486
2 562	**10** 775	**18** 823	**26** 343	**34** 917
3 747	**11** 684	**19** 858	**27** 641	**35** 954
4 259	**12** 76	**20** 164	**28** 168	**36** 202
5 546	**13** 818	**21** 592	**29** 654	**37** 782
6 795	**14** 920	**22** 947	**30** 279	**38** 645
7 173	**15** 259	**23** 409	**31** 391	**39** 817
8 761	**16** 534	**24** 324	**32** 508	**40** 36

5

1 24	**9** 9	**17** 7	**25** 6	**33** 10	**41** 27
2 15	**10** 21	**18** 3	**26** 3	**34** 9	**42** 18
3 33	**11** 12	**19** 10	**27** 11	**35** 1	**43** 30
4 6	**12** 36	**20** 6	**28** 5	**36** 7	**44** 9
5 30	**13** 4	**21** 2	**29** 8	**37** 21	**45** 12
6 3	**14** 9	**22** 11	**30** 2	**38** 3	**46** 33
7 27	**15** 1	**23** 5	**31** 12	**39** 15	**47** 6
8 18	**16** 12	**24** 8	**32** 4	**40** 36	**48** 24

6

1 12, 120	**7** 6, 60	**13** 80	**19** 250	**25** 120 g
2 20, 200	**8** 32, 320	**14** 180	**20** 140	**26** 200
3 44, 440	**9** 15, 150	**15** 240	**21** 300	**27** 240
4 21, 210	**10** 24, 240	**16** 600	**22** 240	**28** 720 ml
5 35, 350	**11** 45, 450	**17** 270	**23** 120	**29** £4.50
6 36, 360	**12** 22, 220	**18** 480	**24** 200	**30** 280

7

1 0·5 cm 4·5 cm 8·5 cm 13·5 cm
2 17 cm 20·5 cm 24·5 cm 27·5 cm
3 10·5 cm **5** 5 cm **7** 8 cm
4 6·5 cm **6** 12·5 cm **8** 9·5 cm
9 A 4·5 cm B 5·5 cm C 4·5 cm D 5·5 cm Perimeter 20 cm
10 X 6·5 cm Y 5·5 cm Z 7·5 cm Perimeter 19·5 cm

9

1 a 10 **b** 12 **5** 50 **9** 20
2 a Dean **b** Bob **6 a** 40 **b** 60 **10** 200
3 8 **7 a** Saturday **b** Tuesday
4 4 **8** 30

10

1 682	**4** 756	**7** 830	**10** 905	**13** 821	**16** 610
2 438	**5** 993	**8** 523	**11** 513	**14** 940	**17** 727
3 262	**6** 836	**9** 765	**12** 980	**15** 754	**18** 1072

11

1 143	**4** 261	**7** 195	**10** 518	**13** 356	**16** 367
2 183	**5** 234	**8** 48	**11** 146	**14** 483	**17** 151
3 227	**6** 380	**9** 374	**12** 353	**15** 179	**18** 685

12

1 20	**9** 16	**17** 4	**25** 16	**33** 20	**41** 10
2 12	**10** 48	**18** 7	**26** 36	**34** 4	**42** 3
3 44	**11** 8	**19** 1	**27** 12	**35** 48	**43** 5
4 28	**12** 36	**20** 12	**28** 44	**36** 28	**44** 9
5 4	**13** 10	**21** 9	**29** 8	**37** 7	**45** 2
6 24	**14** 2	**22** 3	**30** 40	**38** 1	**46** 8
7 32	**15** 8	**23** 11	**31** 24	**39** 6	**47** 4
8 40	**16** 5	**24** 6	**32** 32	**40** 12	**48** 11

13

1 5, 50	**7** 6, 60	**13** 60	**19** 120	**25** 30
2 7, 70	**8** 9, 90	**14** 20	**20** 40	**26** £50
3 6, 60	**9** 11, 110	**15** 90	**21** 90	**27** 20
4 3, 30	**10** 8, 80	**16** 50	**22** 110	**28** 90
5 12, 120	**11** 4, 40	**17** 70	**23** 80	**29** 80
6 8, 80	**12** 6, 60	**18** 20	**24** 50	**30** 70kg

14

1 9:25 pm	**4** 11:05 am	**7** 6:15 pm	**10** 5:43 pm
2 3:20 am	**5** 7:30 am	**8** 10:00 am	**11** 12:23 pm
3 1:45 pm	**6** 11:50 pm	**9** 9:12 am	**12** 11:58 am

15

1 $\frac{1}{2}$ **3** $\frac{1}{10}$ **5** $\frac{2}{3}$ **7** $\frac{2}{5}$ **17** $\frac{1}{10}, \frac{3}{10}, \frac{6}{10}, \frac{9}{10}$ **19** $\frac{1}{6}, \frac{3}{6}, \frac{5}{6}$
2 $\frac{1}{6}$ **4** $\frac{1}{4}$ **6** $\frac{2}{8}$ **8** $\frac{2}{9}$ **18** $\frac{1}{8}, \frac{3}{8}, \frac{5}{8}, \frac{7}{8}$ **20** $\frac{1}{12}, \frac{5}{12}, \frac{8}{12}, \frac{11}{12}$

16

allow +/− 0·1 cm
5 7·0 cm **6** 7·8 cm

17

1 A semicircle	E quadrilateral	**2 a)** B C D E G H
B octagon	F circle	**b)** A F
C rectangle	G square	**c)** C E G
D hexagon	H pentagon	**d)** B G H

18

1 74	**4** 370	**7** 336	**10** 219	**13** 168	**16** £430
2 195	**5** 118	**8** 185	**11** 260	**14** 312	**17** 282
3 116	**6** 144	**9** 164	**12** 460	**15** 128	

19

1 217p	**6** 103p	**11** £9·13	**16** £0·94	**21** 20
2 525p	**7** 849p	**12** £6·70	**17** 10	**22** 100
3 60p	**8** 96p	**13** £1·29	**18** 20	
4 732p	**9** £3·51	**14** £4·65	**19** 4	
5 484p	**10** £0·08	**15** £7·02	**20** 10	

23 Cost	Change	**24** Cost	Change
74p	26p	92p	8p
£5·50	£4·50	£3·49	£1·51
£4·50	50p	£2·30	£7·70
£10·00	0p	£2·87	£2·13
£1·98	2p	£1·79	21p
£2·40	£2·60	£2·05	£2·95

20

1 127 miles	**4** 70 m	**7** 45 cm	**10** 1 m 20 cm
2 300 g	**5** 1300 g	**8** 90 g	**11** 245 g
3 500 ml	**6** 48 litres	**9** 750 ml	**12** 200 ml

21

1 20	**8** 800	**15** 70	**22** 6	**29** 600
2 9	**9** 50	**16** 8	**23** 800	**30** 8
3 500	**10** 7	**17** 30	**24** 70	**31** 2
4 80	**11** 900	**18** 100	**25** 500	**32** 64
5 600	**12** 6	**19** 5	**26** 4	**33** 830
6 4	**13** 40	**20** 400	**27** 96	**34** 7
7 30	**14** 300	**21** 60	**28** 250	**35** 300

22

1 263	**9** 517	**17** 911	**25** 458	459	460	461
2 790	**10** 785	**18** 476	**26** 875	885	895	905
3 911	**11** 933	**19** 723	**27** 597	697	797	897
4 355	**12** 829	**20** 1032	**28** 590	591	592	593
5 600	**13** 191	**21** 820	**29** 803	813	823	833
6 922	**14** 715	**22** 935	**30** 418	518	618	718
7 234	**15** 243	**23** 609				
8 811	**16** 424	**24** 757				

23

1 718	**4** 777	**7** 884	**10** 922	**13** 813	**16** 913
2 401	**5** 847	**8** 984	**11** 612	**14** 546	**17** 940
3 719	**6** 609	**9** 671	**12** 731	**15** 895	**18** 843

24

1 228	**4** 62	**7** 353	**10** 268	**13** 498	**16** 49
2 376	**5** 457	**8** 307	**11** 295	**14** 390	**17** 585
3 316	**6** 184	**9** 45	**12** 694	**15** 264	**18** 156

25

1 250	**8** 720	**15** 360	**22** 150	**29** 160	**36** 350
2 320	**9** 120	**16** 330	**23** 280	**30** 240	**37** 480
3 240	**10** 550	**17** 100	**24** 960	**31** 300	**38** 150
4 100	**11** 270	**18** 640	**25** 360	**32** 140	**39** £180
5 90	**12** 160	**19** 180	**26** 220	**33** 720	**40** 480
6 400	**13** 80	**20** 200	**27** 250	**34** 60	**41** £2.70
7 40	**14** 480	**21** 180	**28** 560	**35** 480	**42** 140

26

1 20	**8** 90	**15** 80	**22** 30	**29** 120	**36** 70
2 60	**9** 70	**16** 70	**23** 70	**30** 90	**37** 60
3 70	**10** 120	**17** 20	**24** 90	**31** 50	**38** 50 g
4 50	**11** 40	**18** 80	**25** 60	**32** 60	**39** 40
5 20	**12** 110	**19** 120	**26** 110	**33** 120	**40** 110
6 80	**13** 30	**20** 30	**27** 80	**34** 60	**41** 30 g
7 40	**14** 110	**21** 120	**28** 50	**35** 90	**42** £40

27

1 5 m	**9** 6 cm	**17** 3500 ml	**25** 790 cm
2 2 kg	**10** 1 litre	**18** 300 m	**26** 700 g
3 10 cm	**11** 4 km	**19** 4600 g	**27** 82 mm
4 4 litres	**12** 9 kg	**20** 190 cm	**28** 1300 ml
5 1000 m	**13** 200 cm	**21** 6 *l* 900 ml	**29** 2 km 800 m
6 5000 g	**14** 7000 ml	**22** 3 cm 7 mm	**30** 8 kg 500 g
7 800 cm	**15** 50 mm	**23** 1 kg 200 g	**31** 4 m 50 cm
8 2000 ml	**16** 3000 g	**24** 5 km 400 m	**32** 0 *l* 100 ml

29

1 110	**9** 120	**17** 120	**25** 70	**33** 80
2 180	**10** 170	**18** 140	**26** 60	**34** 80
3 110	**11** 200	**19** 120	**27** 80	**35** 90
4 130	**12** 180	**20** 180	**28** 70	**36** 50
5 120	**13** 100	**21** 60	**29** 90	**37** 70
6 150	**14** 150	**22** 90	**30** 70	**38** 90
7 190	**15** 160	**23** 50	**31** 80	**39** 40
8 130	**16** 140	**24** 50	**32** 70	**40** 50

30

1 10,11,21	**3** 4,8,29	**5** 3,18,32	**7** 23,27,11	**9** 12,12,20
2 12,12,24	**4** 9,13,33	**6** 5,6,11	**8** 9,6,26	**10** 12,7,19

31

1 32	**9** 24	**17** 1	**25** 5	**33** 9	**41** 96
2 80	**10** 40	**18** 7	**26** 1	**34** 6	**42** 24
3 8	**11** 96	**19** 5	**27** 10	**35** 3	**43** 40
4 64	**12** 56	**20** 12	**28** 8	**36** 12	**44** 64
5 88	**13** 6	**21** 4	**29** 2	**37** 56	**45** 80
6 16	**14** 11	**22** 10	**30** 7	**38** 88	**46** 8
7 72	**15** 3	**23** 2	**31** 4	**39** 48	**47** 72
8 48	**16** 9	**24** 8	**32** 11	**40** 16	**48** 32

32

1 136	**4** 490	**7** 96	**10** 325	**13** 472	**16** 744 g
2 150	**5** 512	**8** 162	**11** 388	**14** 235	**17** 300
3 201	**6** 344	**9** 624	**12** 117	**15** 258	

33

1 34	**5** 19	**9** 32	**13** 13	**17** 28
2 13	**6** 24	**10** 16	**14** 17	**18** 37
3 20	**7** 15	**11** 19	**15** 45	**19** 19p
4 23	**8** 26	**12** 23	**16** 18	**20** 27

34

1 1.4 cm	5.8 cm	9.2 cm	12.7 cm
2 15.5 cm	18.1 cm	22.9 cm	28.3 cm
3 9.5 cm	**5** 12.2 cm	**7** 10.9 cm	
4 5.3 cm	**6** 6.8 cm		

35

1 7	**7** 8	**13** 6	**19** 11	**25** 5	**31** £30
2 4	**8** 10	**14** 7	**20** 9	**26** 10	**32** £12
3 9	**9** 9	**15** 9	**21** 6	**27** 3	**33** 400 g
4 12	**10** 3	**16** 12	**22** 8	**28** 6	**34** 200 g
5 6	**11** 5	**17** 9	**23** 12	**29** 12	**35** 100 g
6 11	**12** 10	**18** 5	**24** 8	**30** £6	

36

2 $\frac{4}{8}$	**5** $\frac{6}{10}$	**8** $\frac{3}{6}$	**11** $\frac{6}{8}$	**14** $\frac{10}{12}$
3 $\frac{8}{10}$	**6** $\frac{2}{8}$	**9** $\frac{2}{4}$	**12** $\frac{4}{6}$	**15** $\frac{8}{8}$
4 $\frac{9}{12}$	**7** $\frac{6}{9}$	**10** $\frac{2}{12}$	**13** $\frac{2}{8}$	**16** $\frac{4}{12}$

37

1 6 o'clock	**7** 1 o'clock	**13** three quarter
2 3 o'clock	**8** 10 o'clock	**14** right angle
3 12 o'clock	**9** half	**15** three quarter
4 9 o'clock	**10** three quarter	**16** right angle
5 4 o'clock	**11** right angle	
6 7 o'clock	**12** half	

17 A right angle	**18** D right angle	**19** H smaller
B smaller	E smaller	I larger
C smaller	F right angle	J right angle
	G larger	K right angle

38

1 7	**4** 8	**7** 90 miles	**10** 40
2 12	**5** 2	**8** 5	**11** 25
3 12	**6** 30	**9** £6	**12** 5

39

1 361 m	**10** 833 km	**19** £268	**28** £344
2 824 g	**11** 766 ml	**20** 144 km	**29** 168 m
3 £477	**12** £441	**21** 928 kg	**30** 682 ml
4 241 km	**13** 924 m	**22** £335	**31** £541
5 791 ml	**14** 857 g	**23** 776 m	**32** 236 km
6 £954	**15** £779	**24** 419 ml	**33** 603 kg
7 328 m	**16** 542 km	**25** £499	**34** £495
8 602 kg	**17** 610 ml	**26** 777 km	**35** 249 m
9 £225	**18** £988	**27** 555 g	**36** 164 ml

40

1 7:50 am	**4** 5:40 am	**7** 8:45 pm	**10** 7:14 am
2 3:15 pm	**5** 6:57 pm	**8** 12:22 pm	**11** 10:59 pm
3 11:25 pm	**6** 10:08 am	**9** 2:36 am	**12** 4:03 pm

41

1 300 + 70 + 6	**7** 200 + 50 + 7	**13** 7	**19** 9	**25** 2
2 800 + 40 + 8	**8** 700 + 20 + 9	**14** 81	**20** 74	**26** 95
3 500 + 80 + 3	**9** 100 + 30 + 4	**15** 700	**21** 300	**27** 240
4 900 + 60 + 1	**10** 500 + 60 + 9	**16** 260	**22** 10	**28** 80
5 400 + 10 + 5	**11** 200 + 90 + 6	**17** 40	**23** 120	
6 600 + 30 + 2	**12** 700 + 10 + 8	**18** 506	**24** 509	

42

1 20	**5** 32	**9** 24	**13** 28	**17** 48	**21** 36
2 32	**6** 56	**10** 80	**14** 40	**18** 72	**22** 48
3 150	**7** 300	**11** 350	**15** 200	**19** 250	**23** 400
4 500	**8** 900	**12** 400	**16** 800	**20** 600	**24** 1000

25 4	8	12	16	20	24	28	32	36	40
26 8	16	24	32	40	48	56	64	72	80
27 50	100	150	200	250	300	350	400	450	500
28 100	200	300	400	500	600	700	800	900	1000
29 53	153	253	353	453	553	653	753	853	953
30 6	56	106	156	206	256	306	356	406	456

43

1 60	**7** 81	**13** 54	**19** 29	**25** 68	**31** 39
2 30	**8** 26	**14** 37	**20** 58	**26** 26	**32** 65
3 95	**9** 90	**15** 93	**21** 46	**27** 54	
4 45	**10** 40	**16** 18	**22** 45	**28** 79	
5 62	**11** 75	**17** 77	**23** 57	**29** 84	
6 9	**12** 15	**18** 66	**24** 84	**30** 47	

44

1 63	**5** 27	**9** 81	**13** 114	**17** 27	**21** 68
2 91	**6** 69	**10** 106	**14** 83	**18** 45	**22** 49
3 124	**7** 78	**11** 72	**15** 164	**19** 14	**23** 35
4 142	**8** 66	**12** 145	**16** 126	**20** 86	**24** 88

45

1 4	**10** 30	**19** 100	**28** 15	**37** 24	**46** 32
2 16	**11** 15	**20** 70	**29** 33	**38** 4	**47** 72
3 22	**12** 60	**21** 90	**30** 24	**39** 48	**48** 56
4 6	**13** 1	**22** 4	**31** 6	**40** 2	**49** 10
5 5	**14** 9	**23** 12	**32** 3	**41** 11	**50** 8
6 9	**15** 7	**24** 8	**33** 9	**42** 7	**51** 12
7 8	**16** 55	**25** 20	**34** 3	**43** 20	**52** 24
8 24	**17** 50	**26** 60	**35** 36	**44** 32	**53** 88
9 14	**18** 40	**27** 110	**36** 21	**45** 36	**54** 48

46

1 43	**5** 12	**9** 29	**13** 14	**17** 20
2 16	**6** 18	**10** 17	**14** 35	**18** 47
3 14	**7** 25	**11** 18	**15** 29	**19** 18
4 13	**8** 24	**12** 19	**16** 17	**20** 39

47

1 1·5 *l*, 4·5 *l*	**5** 200 g, 600 g	**9** 150 g	**13** 8 *l*, 16 *l*
2 0·5 *l*, 2·5 *l*	**6** 1 kg, 5 kg	**10** 5 kg	**14** 150 ml, 450 ml
3 40 ml, 70 ml	**7** 50 g, 350 g	**11** 20 g	**15** 15 *l*, 35 *l*
4 75 ml, 175 ml	**8** 0·5 kg, 1·5 kg	**12** 1·5 kg	**16** 250 ml, 1250 ml

48

1 55 kg	**4** 40 g	**7** 1 kg 300 g	**10** 120 kg
2 36 m	**5** 343 m	**8** 20 cm	**11** 65 miles
3 20 ml	**6** 750 ml	**9** 103 litres	**12** 350 ml

49

1 a 8 **b** 16	**5** 54	**9** 4
2 a grey **b** black	**6** 30	**10 a** 20 **b** 32
3 2	**7** 16	**11** 68
4 10	**8** 4	**12** 8,9

50

1 35	**7** 119	**13** 23	**19** 428	**25** 36	**31** 646
2 88	**8** 784	**14** 45	**20** 285	**26** 65	**32** 282
3 53	**9** 337	**15** 59	**21** 763	**27** 48	**33** 417
4 71	**10** 875	**16** 28	**22** 569	**28** 44	**34** 590
5 16	**11** 442	**17** 42	**23** 336	**29** 29	**35** 753
6 44	**12** 257	**18** 57	**24** 812	**30** 73	**36** 838

51

1 114	**5** 135	**9** 224	**13** 202
2 157	**6** 79 kg	**10** 75p	**14** 26
3 585 g	**7** 482	**11** 88	**15** 172
4 48	**8** 55 cm	**12** 70	**16** 68

52

1 108	**5** 116	**9** 465	**13** 17	**17** 13	**21** 46
2 200	**6** 222	**10** 272	**14** 25	**18** 24	**22** 15
3 76	**7** 368	**11** 177	**15** 19	**19** 19	**23** 18
4 235	**8** 150	**12** 664	**16** 34	**20** 16	**24** 27

53

1 28	**5** 9	**9** 6	**13** 120	**17** 20p
2 8	**6** 60p	**10** 400	**14** 60 g	**18** 240
3 £6·00	**7** 30	**11** 12	**15** 200 ml	**19** 35
4 £10	**8** 22	**12** 36	**16** 240	**20** 45

54

1 60	**7** 18	**13** 12	**19** 13	**25** 2	**31** 6:00
2 24	**8** 44	**14** 46	**20** 3	**26** 15	**32** 6:15
3 25	**9** 7	**15** 5	**21** 11	**27** 55	
4 40	**10** 31	**16** 16	**22** 18	**28** 3:10	
5 10	**11** 23	**17** 9	**23** 6	**29** 2:00	
6 55	**12** 59	**18** 20	**24** 23	**30** 37	

55

1 $\frac{1}{4}$	**5** $\frac{2}{5}$	**9** $\frac{2}{4}$	**13** $\frac{3}{9}$	**17** $\frac{2}{5}$
2 $\frac{3}{6}$	**6** $\frac{1}{8}$	**10** $\frac{6}{10}$	**14** $\frac{1}{7}$	**18** $\frac{4}{8}$
3 $\frac{2}{3}$	**7** $\frac{2}{3}$	**11** $\frac{3}{5}$	**15** $\frac{1}{6}$	
4 $\frac{6}{10}$	**8** $\frac{7}{8}$	**12** $\frac{7}{12}$	**16** $\frac{5}{10}$	

56

1 $\frac{2}{6}$	**5** $\frac{5}{8}$	**9** $\frac{9}{10}$	**13** $\frac{1}{12}, \frac{4}{12}, \frac{11}{12}$
2 $\frac{1}{2}$	**6** $\frac{4}{5}$	**10** $\frac{1}{10}, \frac{1}{4}, \frac{1}{2}$	**14** $\frac{2}{8}, \frac{2}{7}, \frac{2}{3}$
3 $\frac{7}{12}$	**7** $\frac{4}{7}$	**11** $\frac{1}{5}, \frac{3}{5}, \frac{4}{5}$	**15** $\frac{6}{9}, \frac{7}{9}, \frac{8}{9}$
4 $\frac{3}{7}$	**8** $\frac{2}{3}$	**12** $\frac{5}{12}, \frac{5}{8}, \frac{5}{6}$	

57

1 a) hemisphere
b) cylinder
c) cone
d) sphere

2

	Shape	F	E	V
A	hexagonal prism	8	18	12
B	triangular based pyramid	4	6	4
C	cube	6	12	8
D	pentagonal prism	7	15	10
E	square based pyramid	5	8	5
F	octagonal prism	10	24	16
G	triangular prism	5	9	6
H	cuboid	6	12	8

58

1 obtuse	**4** right angle	**7** A acute	G acute
2 right angle	**5** obtuse	B obtuse	H obtuse
3 acute	**6** acute	C right angle	I acute
		D right angle	J right angle
		E obtuse	K obtuse
		F acute	L right angle

59

1 £18	**4** 60 ml	**7** 400 ml	**10** £120
2 30 g	**5** 90 km	**8** 40 litres	**11** £4·80
3 36 cm	**6** 280 g	**9** 30 cm	**12** 60 kg

60

1 450	**7** 500, 9	**13** 714	**19** 363	**25** 24	**31** 153
2 672	**8** 50, 4	**14** 303	**20** 85	**26** 40	**32** 431
3 384	**9** 38	**15** 968	**21** 701	**27** 200	**33** 826
4 907	**10** 210	**16** 592	**22** 387	**28** 36	**34** 642
5 40	**11** 62	**17** 626	**23** 520	**29** 64	**35** 939
6 700	**12** 300	**18** 957	**24** 854	**30** 350	**36** 795

61

1 192	**11** 698	**21** 160	**31** 64	**41** 8	**51** 238
2 336	**12** 175	**22** 115	**32** 59	**42** 9	**52** 445
3 802	**13** 444	**23** 151	**33** 12	**43** 12	**53** 85
4 1038	**14** 69	**24** 133	**34** 33	**44** 8	**54** 69
5 541	**15** 382	**25** 25	**35** 36	**45** 90	**55** 141
6 934	**16** 36	**26** 57	**36** 40	**46** 120	**56** 124
7 816	**17** 81	**27** 46	**37** 600	**47** 70	**57** 70
8 740	**18** 94	**28** 19	**38** 210	**48** 60	**58** 110
9 668	**19** 132	**29** 35	**39** 240	**49** 15	**59** 240
10 383	**20** 123	**30** 78	**40** 720	**50** 60	**60** 560

62

1 462	**5** 710	**9** 671	**13** 228	**17** 117	**21** 15
2 920	**6** 652	**10** 128	**14** 180	**18** 272	**22** 17
3 567	**7** 369	**11** 225	**15** 216	**19** 26	**23** 39
4 844	**8** 364	**12** 514	**16** 480	**20** 24	**24** 14

63

1 A $\frac{1}{5}$ **B** $\frac{4}{5}$	**9** $\frac{1}{8}$ $\frac{1}{5}$ $\frac{1}{3}$	**17** $\frac{6}{10}$	**25** 9
2 C $\frac{2}{10}$ **D** $\frac{7}{10}$	**10** $\frac{3}{7}$ $\frac{4}{7}$ $\frac{6}{7}$	**18** $\frac{5}{10}$	**26** 2
3 $\frac{1}{4}$ $\frac{2}{8}$	**11** $\frac{7}{10}$	**19** $\frac{7}{10}$	**27** 12
4 $\frac{4}{6}$ $\frac{2}{3}$	**12** $\frac{1}{6}$	**20** $\frac{5}{10}$	**28** 8
5 $\frac{4}{6}$	**13** $\frac{3}{5}$	**21** 8	**29** 5
6 $\frac{2}{3}$	**14** $\frac{3}{9}$	**22** 6	**30** 7
7 $\frac{7}{8}$	**15** $\frac{5}{8}$	**23** 7	**31** 12
8 $\frac{5}{9}$	**16** $\frac{6}{12}$	**24** 10	**32** 6

64

1 40 mm	**6** 90 mins.
2 200 cm	**7** 2 cm 7 mm
3 5000 m	**8** 5 m 40 cm
4 8000 ml	**9** 0 km 700 m
5 3000 g	**10** 4 *l* 800 ml

11 2 kg 500 g
12 5 mins.
13 500 g, 1500 g
14 200 ml, 800 ml
15 AB 2 cm 7 mm
BC 3 cm 6 mm
AC 4 cm 5 mm
Perimeter 10 cm 8 mm
16 2:50pm
17 4:25 am
18 12:07 am
19 5:40 pm
20 45 mins., 55 mins.
21 £1·44, 56p

65

1 123
2 3500 ml
3 £3·50
4 403
5 35 cm
6 3 eighths
7 12
8 48
9 36
10 5, 8
11 240
12 3 mins, 20 secs
13 £85
14 9
15 90
16 44
17 347
18 £2·30
19 70
20 14 cm

YEAR 4 PRACTICE WORKBOOK ANSWERS

1

1 395
2 4142
3 937
4 2510
5 1068
6 6704
7 5871
8 3326
9 7083
10 9209
11 one thousand five hundred and twenty-four
12 nine hunded and sixty-one
13 seven thousand one hundred and eight
14 nine thousand two hundred and thirty-five
15 five thousand and seventy-three
16 two thousand eight hundred and forty-nine
17 eight thousand three hundred
18 six thousand four hundred and seventeen
19 three thousand and two
20 nine thousand and thirty-six

2

1 700
2 90
3 2000
4 40
5 500
6 6000
7 20
8 6
9 600
10 50
11 9000
12 800
13 5
14 8000
15 70
16 7314
17 847
18 7563
19 9239
20 7135
21 7806
22 2041
23 3018
24 5092
25 7485
26 −400
27 +20
28 −6000
29 −50
30 +900
31 +5000
32 −700
33 +80
34 +4000
35 +7900

3

1 3224
2 6427
3 5403
4 1882
5 6780
6 218
7 1796
8 9010
9 7677
10 6661
11 2679
12 4432
13 5398
14 5507
15 2315
16 1885
17 2820
18 3364
19 4339
20 5570
21 1535
22 4643
23 7218
24 4932
25 1035
26 401
27 294
28 7966
29 5580
30 7357
31 5766
32 4407
33 5373
34 9328
35 2506
36 5914

4

1 5483
2 8120
3 2393
4 6005
5 3832
6 7035
7 6021
8 9725
9 4280
10 8701
11 8132
12 9503
13 3103
14 5482
15 7550
16 8763
17 5702
18 8141

5

1 2846
2 1574
3 7145
4 903
5 1195
6 4539
7 648
8 1375
9 3963
10 2809
11 2575
12 962
13 6033
14 3571
15 1498
16 4668
17 1238
18 2903

6

1 42
2 12
3 30
4 60
5 24
6 72
7 0
8 48
9 66
10 36
11 54
12 18
13 4
14 1
15 7
16 11
17 8
18 2
19 10
20 6
21 3
22 12
23 5
24 9
25 10
26 6
27 3
28 9
29 5
30 2
31 8
32 11
33 12
34 0
35 7
36 4
37 24
38 54
39 12
40 36
41 66
42 18
43 42
44 60
45 30
46 6
47 72
48 48

7

1 $\frac{2}{4}$
2 $\frac{3}{9}$
3 $\frac{10}{12}$
4 $\frac{6}{8}$
5 $\frac{6}{9}$
6 $\frac{4}{8}$
7 $\frac{2}{8}$
8 $\frac{8}{10}$
9 $\frac{2}{12}$
10 $\frac{4}{10}$
11 $\frac{3}{12}$
12 $\frac{4}{6}$
13 $\frac{5}{10}$
14 $\frac{6}{8}$
15 $\frac{6}{9}$
16 $\frac{8}{10}$

8

1 4:17 pm
2 3:43 am
3 10:01 pm
4 10:25 am
5 1:52 pm
6 12:38 am
7 06:09
8 12:14
9 02:57
10 18:33
11 08:21
12 23:41

9

No.	Time in words	12-Hour Clock	24-Hour Clock		
1	25 mins. to 10	9:35 am	09:35	**1**	25
2	5 past 10	10:05 pm	22:05	**2**	55
3	8 mins. to 5	4:52 am	04:52	**3**	8
4	10 past 1	1:10 pm	13:10	**4**	50
5	19 mins. to 12	11:41 am	11:41	**5**	19
6	23 mins. past 2	2:23 pm	14:23	**6**	37
7	8 mins. past 5	5:08 am	05:08	**7**	52
8	3 mins. to 9	8:57 pm	20:57	**8**	3
9	26 mins. to 2	1:34 am	01:34	**9**	26
10	12 mins. past 12	12:12 pm	12:12	**10**	48
11	14 mins. to 4	3:46 pm	15:46	**11**	14
12	29 mins. past 7	7:29 am	07:29	**12**	31

10

1 CFIK
2 CK
3 ADGL
4 ADG
5 BEHJ
6 BDHI
7 ACEFGJKL
8 ABDGJ
9 DE
10 ABGHJL
11 ACEFGIKL
12 AF

11

1 35
2 56
3 7
4 84
5 49
6 21
7 70
8 28
9 14
10 77
11 42
12 63
13 4
14 10
15 2
16 7
17 9
18 6
19 11
20 0
21 12
22 3
23 8
24 5
25 6
26 11
27 3
28 9
29 2
30 8
31 5
32 12
33 4
34 10
35 1
36 7
37 49
38 28
39 0
40 70
41 42
42 77
43 56
44 21
45 35
46 14
47 63
48 84

12

1 2192
2 2418
3 3174
4 2992
5 2555
6 3435
7 2256
8 1264
9 1743
10 17
11 35
12 24
13 78
14 26
15 29
16 35
17 17
18 79

13

1 0·3, 0·7
2 0·12, 0·16
3 0·2
4 0·58
5 0·5
6 0·01
7 0·74
8 0·25
9 0·2
10 0·9
11 0·75
12 0·06
13 0·5
14 0·32
15 $\frac{95}{100}$
16 $\frac{4}{100}$
17 $\frac{37}{100}$
18 $\frac{1}{2}$ or $\frac{5}{10}$
19 $\frac{82}{100}$
20 $\frac{1}{10}$
21 $\frac{3}{4}$ or $\frac{75}{100}$
22 $\frac{9}{100}$
23 $\frac{1}{4}$ or $\frac{25}{100}$
24 $\frac{53}{100}$
25 $\frac{6}{10}$ or $\frac{3}{5}$
26 $\frac{41}{100}$
27 $\frac{4}{100}$
28 $\frac{2}{100}$
29 $\frac{5}{10}$
30 $\frac{8}{10}$
31 $\frac{6}{10}$
32 $\frac{8}{100}$
33 $\frac{5}{100}$
34 $\frac{2}{10}$
35 $\frac{3}{100}$
36 $\frac{4}{10}$
37 $\frac{7}{10}$
38 $\frac{9}{100}$

14

1 4	**9** 3·6	**17** 2·5	**25** 2000	**33** 2600
2 11·5	**10** 0·2	**18** 0·4	**26** 20	**34** 9800
3 0·3	**11** 5·8	**19** 6	**27** 300	**35** 500
4 7·9	**12** 9	**20** 3·8	**28** 850	**36** 3000
5 10·1	**13** 1·3	**21** 32	**29** 4000	**37** 5200
6 5·4	**14** 0·9	**22** 6	**30** 1300	**38** 1900
7 2	**15** 4·7	**23** 120	**31** 700	**39** 7000
8 0·7	**16** 8	**24** 50	**32** 6400	**40** 100

16

1 36	**9** 27	**17** 1	**25** 7	**33** 6	**41** 99
2 99	**10** 63	**18** 5	**26** 5	**34** 3	**42** 54
3 18	**11** 45	**19** 12	**27** 0	**35** 11	**43** 9
4 81	**12** 108	**20** 7	**28** 12	**36** 8	**44** 81
5 54	**13** 10	**21** 4	**29** 9	**37** 90	**45** 18
6 0	**14** 3	**22** 2	**30** 4	**38** 27	**46** 63
7 90	**15** 6	**23** 9	**31** 10	**39** 72	**47** 36
8 72	**16** 8	**24** 11	**32** 2	**40** 45	**48** 108

17

1 270	**9** 3000	**17** 7	**25** 700	**33** 3200
2 4200	**10** 7200	**18** 50	**26** 9	**34** 360
3 1600	**11** 30	**19** 6	**27** 800	**35** 1400
4 480	**12** 900	**20** 90	**28** 50	**36** 420
5 350	**13** 600	**21** 600	**29** 6	**37** 4500
6 3200	**14** 90	**22** 80	**30** 40	**38** 5600
7 1800	**15** 300	**23** 5	**31** 210	**39** 300
8 360	**16** 80	**24** 90	**32** 4800	**40** 7200

18

1 84	**5** 240	**9** 132	**13** 42
2 80	**6** 9	**10** 70	**14** 11, 11
3 54	**7** £1000	**11** 72	**15** 3200 g
4 40	**8** 3 g	**12** 5	**16** 1500 ml

19

1 Length 6·5 cm	**2** 8 cm^2, 14 cm
Width 3·3 cm	**3** 10 cm^2, 18 cm
Perimeter 19·6 cm	**4** 12 cm^2, 16 cm

20

1 CAB **2** DEF **3** HIG **4** KMJL **5** ONP **6** TQRS

7 A right angle	H obtuse	O acute
B obtuse	I obtuse	P right angle
C acute	J obtuse	Q right angle
D acute	K acute	R obtuse
E right angle	L obtuse	S obtuse
F obtuse	M right angle	T acute
G obtuse	N acute	

21

1 24	**9** 115	**17** 1900	**25** −2
2 70	**10** 132	**18** 2454	**26** 4
3 72	**11** 42	**19** 2038	**27** −5
4 56	**12** 45	**20** 5607	**28** 6
5 27	**13** 1310	**21** 6255	**29** −4
6 56	**14** 4320	**22** 7750	**30** 0
7 72	**15** 9190	**23** −3	**31** −1
8 54	**16** 8700	**24** 1	**32** 2

22

1 1720	**10** 9220	**19** 3900	**28** 8000
2 2440	**11** 3500	**20** 8000	**29** 2000
3 5400	**12** 1600	**21** 1000	**30** 7000
4 8670	**13** 7300	**22** 5000	**31** 760
5 3830	**14** 4300	**23** 4000	**32** 550
6 4070	**15** 6900	**24** 5000	**33** 1300
7 6500	**16** 2200	**25** 3000	**34** 860
8 2180	**17** 8600	**26** 6000	**35** 210
9 7950	**18** 6700	**27** 9000	**36** 480

23

1 130	**10** 600	**19** 140	**28** 900
2 120	**11** 700	**20** 60	**29** 1400
3 170	**12** 900	**21** 80	**30** 800
4 70	**13** 72	**22** 70	**31** 57
5 90	**14** 46	**23** 70	**32** 8
6 60	**15** 93	**24** 40	**33** 65
7 1600	**16** 39	**25** 500	**34** 16
8 1200	**17** 85	**26** 600	**35** 71
9 1100	**18** 24	**27** 1200	**36** 49

24

1 7562	**5** 2368	**9** 9011	**13** 4153	**17** 5833
2 5215	**6** 5669	**10** 4527	**14** 6513	**18** 4585
3 8045	**7** 5352	**11** 3654	**15** 7007	
4 2353	**8** 9256	**12** 1373	**16** 3129	

25

1 35	**10** 16	**19** 24	**28** 42	**37** 45
2 4	**11** 32	**20** 54	**29** 21	**38** 63
3 60	**12** 33	**21** 12	**30** 56	**39** 81
4 11	**13** 12	**22** 7	**31** 5	**40** 4
5 9	**14** 7	**23** 3	**32** 7	**41** 6
6 10	**15** 0	**24** 12	**33** 11	**42** 12
7 40	**16** 14	**25** 30	**34** 28	**43** 90
8 48	**17** 72	**26** 48	**35** 84	**44** 27
9 50	**18** 18	**27** 36	**36** 63	**45** 72

26

1 55	**9** 77	**17** 2	**25** 2	**33** 0	**41** 77
2 110	**10** 22	**18** 5	**26** 7	**34** 10	**42** 22
3 33	**11** 121	**19** 10	**27** 12	**35** 5	**43** 55
4 88	**12** 66	**20** 7	**28** 4	**36** 9	**44** 132
5 11	**13** 9	**21** 3	**29** 11	**37** 33	**45** 44
6 99	**14** 1	**22** 8	**30** 6	**38** 110	**46** 121
7 44	**15** 6	**23** 12	**31** 3	**39** 88	**47** 11
8 132	**16** 11	**24** 4	**32** 8	**40** 66	**48** 99

27

1 3836	**5** 4870	**9** 1722	**13** 25	**17** 36	**21** 38
2 4764	**6** 4232	**10** 7614	**14** 17	**18** 58	**22** 65
3 1314	**7** 5572	**11** 2925	**15** 36	**19** 47	**23** 36
4 3375	**8** 1860	**12** 3736	**16** 19	**20** 69	**24** 49

28

1 £0·73	**10** 0·7 cm	**19** 0·2 kg, 0·7 kg	**28** £50
2 £1·26	**11** 29·3 cm	**20** 0·3 m, 0·8 m	**29** 6p
3 £0·41	**12** 1·5 cm	**21** 8p	**30** 5 kg
4 £5·90	**13** 3·38 m	**22** 50p	**31** 400 g
5 £18·05	**14** 9·7 m	**23** 80p	**32** 20 g
6 £0·08	**15** 0·06 m	**24** 9 cm	**33** 50p
7 6·2 cm	**16** 24·51 m	**25** 60 cm	**34** 3p
8 0·9 cm	**17** 0·19 m	**26** 7 m	**35** £1
9 10·4 cm	**18** 7·02 m	**27** 90p	**36** 600 m

37 20 km
38 40 m
39 £0·99 £1·00 £1·01 £1·02
40 0·1 m 0·12 m 0·14 m 0·16 m

29

1 20
2 9
3 75
4 38
5 50
6 500
7 37
8 155
9 600
10 6000
11 2100
12 420
13 1200
14 3960
15 10
16 5800
17 700
18 2590
19 4000
20 250
21 5·1
22 1
23 0·6
24 9·3
25 3·45
26 0·8
27 8·2
28 4·03
29 1·78
30 7·2
31 0·02
32 5·46
33 0·5
34 2·34
35 6·05
36 0·9
37 3·22
38 0·8
39 1·6
40 0·07

30

1 A quadrilateral
B trapezium
C square
D isosceles triangle
E equilateral triangle
F rhombus

31

1 B
2 K
3 Q
4 X
5 S
6 H
7 N
8 C
9 (3, 4)
10 (5, 0)
11 (1, 2)
12 (0, 5)
13 (4, 6)
14 (6, 1)
15 (2, 3)
16 (3, 2)
17 (4, 4)(5, 0)(2, 1)(0, 6)(6, 3)
18 (3, 5)(1, 0)(6, 0)(2, 6)
19 (6, 3)(0, 1)(4, 4)(5, 0)(2, 5)
20 (3, 4)(2, 5)(5, 2)(5, 2)(0, 1)
21 R
22 T
23 F
24 Q
25 H
26 W
27 K
28 Z

32

1 24
2 84
3 132
4 48
5 96
6 36
7 120
8 72
9 0
10 108
11 60
12 144
13 5
14 8
15 3
16 10
17 1
18 12
19 4
20 9
21 6
22 2
23 11
24 7
25 6
26 1
27 12
28 8
29 2
30 7
31 5
32 11
33 3
34 10
35 8
36 4
37 120
38 60
39 84
40 0
41 36
42 96
43 144
44 48
45 108
46 24
47 72
48 132

33

1 Area 6 cm^2 Perimeter 14 cm
2 Area 8 cm^2 Perimeter 14 cm
3 Area 40 cm^2 Perimeter 26 cm
4 Area 66 cm^2 Perimeter 34 cm
5 Area 49 cm^2 Perimeter 28 cm
6 Area 15 cm^2 Perimeter 16 cm
7 sides 10 cm Area 100 cm^2
8 side 4 cm Perimeter 38 cm
9

Length	Width	Area	Perimeter
10	4	40	28
7	2	14	18
14	5	70	38
9	9	81	36
20	10	200	60
12	8	96	40

10 width 2·5 cm

35

1 Bina
2 46
3 54
4 Deva
5 Music
6 Calvin
7 2
8 a) Ashley, Bina, Calvin, Fran
b) Ashley, Deva, Errol, Fran
9 English
10 Deva
11 History

36

1 80 g
2 240 g
3 560 g
4 40 m
5 80 m
6 160 m
7 50 ml
8 100 ml
9 250 ml
10 £15
11 £60
12 £300
13 £70
14 25 g
15 9p
16 50 m
17 6 litres
18 12 km
19 8 cm
20 30 kg
21 180 ml
22 £32
23 25 mm
24 450 g
25 36p
26 18 kg
27 330 m
28 20 litres

37

1 $\frac{1}{5}\ \frac{2}{5}\ \frac{3}{5}\ \frac{4}{5}\ 1$
2 $\frac{1}{9}\ \frac{2}{9}\ \frac{3}{9}\ \frac{4}{9}\ \frac{5}{9}\ \frac{6}{9}\ \frac{7}{9}\ \frac{8}{9}\ 1$
3 $\frac{1}{8}\ \frac{2}{8}\ \frac{3}{8}\ \frac{4}{8}\ \frac{5}{8}\ \frac{6}{8}\ \frac{7}{8}\ 1$
4 $\frac{1}{12}\ \frac{2}{12}\ \frac{3}{12}\ \frac{4}{12}\ \frac{5}{12}\ \frac{6}{12}\ \frac{7}{12}\ \frac{8}{12}\ \frac{9}{12}\ \frac{10}{12}\ \frac{11}{12}\ 1$
5 $1\ \frac{3}{4}\ \frac{2}{4}\ \frac{1}{4}\ 0$
6 $1\ \frac{5}{6}\ \frac{4}{6}\ \frac{3}{6}\ \frac{2}{6}\ \frac{1}{6}\ 0$
7 $1\ \frac{9}{10}\ \frac{8}{10}\ \frac{7}{10}\ \frac{6}{10}\ \frac{5}{10}\ \frac{4}{10}\ \frac{3}{10}\ \frac{2}{10}\ \frac{1}{10}\ 0$
8 $1\ \frac{6}{7}\ \frac{5}{7}\ \frac{4}{7}\ \frac{3}{7}\ \frac{2}{7}\ \frac{1}{7}\ 0$
9 5·6 5·7 5·8 5·9 6 6·1
10 0·01 0·02 0·03 0·04 0·05 0·06
11 0·93 1·03 1·13 1·23 1·33 1·43
12 1·77 1·78 1·79 1·8 1·81 1·82
13 2·4 2·3 2·2 2·1 2 1·9
14 1·69 1·68 1·67 1·66 1·65 1·64
15 4·09 3·99 3·89 3·79 3·69 3·59
16 2·99 2·98 2·97 2·96 2·95 2·94

38

1 640 m
2 1·5 litres
3 1·82 m
4 800 g
5 £3·52
6 0·9 m
7 3·45 kg
8 2·8 cm
9 1·55 litres
10 £2·40

39

1 £4·20
2 £1·73
3 20p
4 £9·13
5 £1·80
6 £1·25
7 45p
8 £4·30
9 £5·45
10 £6·75
11 £0·80
12 £4·30

40

1 9041
2 1110 ml
3 £4373
4 67
5 3348
6 2834
7 £456
8 5416

41

1 48
2 87
3 29
4 96
5 15
6 60
7 34
8 51
9 8
10 79
11 43
12 80
13 26
14 97
15 19
16 64
17 31
18 55
19 4
20 72
21 48
22 17
23 23
24 99
25 XXXV
26 XXVIII
27 XC
28 LVI
29 LXXXIII
30 XLIV
31 XII
32 IX
33 LXXVII
34 XXIV
35 LXXXI
36 XXXIX
37 LXVI
38 XCIII
39 LVIII
40 XLII
41 VI
42 XX
43 LXXV
44 LXXXIV
45 XXXVII
46 LIX
47 LXIII
48 XCVIII

42

1 73
2 91
3 37
4 36
5 78
6 21
7 124
8 101
9 49
10 66
11 85
12 98
13 133
14 122
15 97
16 58
17 75
18 67
19 29
20 55

21 29 **25** 79 **29** 102 **33** 44
22 15 **26** 86 **30** 144 **34** 73
23 67 **27** 58 **31** 87 **35** 182
24 94 **28** 73 **32** 99 **36** 123

43

1 48 **2** 30 **3** 108 **4** 9 **5** 12 **6** 7 **7** 48 **8** 18 **9** 56
10 84 **11** 42 **12** 27 **13** 8 **14** 11 **15** 7 **16** 5 **17** 63 **18** 36
19 88 **20** 28 **21** 72 **22** 9 **23** 12 **24** 7 **25** 121 **26** 144 **27** 64
28 0 **29** 45 **30** 48 **31** 12 **32** 9 **33** 8 **34** 24 **35** 35 **36** 72
37 22 **38** 63 **39** 96 **40** 1 **41** 9 **42** 6 **43** 66 **44** 21 **45** 108

44

1 315 **2** 114 **3** 158 **4** 208
5 438 **6** 188 **7** 315 **8** 203
9 280 **10** 696 **11** 150 **12** 612
13 172 **14** 518 **15** 294 **16** 280
17 171 **18** 846 **19** 476 **20** 245
21 516 **22** 156 **23** 752 **24** 243

45

1 $\frac{6}{10}$ **2** $\frac{3}{4}$ **3** $\frac{4}{7}$ **4** $\frac{1}{3}$ **5** $\frac{2}{11}$ **6** $\frac{5}{8}$
7 $\frac{2}{5}$ **8** $\frac{3}{12}$ **9** $\frac{2}{6}$ **10** $\frac{4}{9}$ **11** $\frac{1}{4}$ **12** $\frac{3}{10}$
13 $\frac{3}{8}$ **14** $\frac{1}{3}$ **15** $\frac{5}{9}$ **16** $\frac{9}{12}$ **17** $\frac{4}{5}$ **18** $\frac{6}{6}$
19 7 **20** 11 **21** 10 **22** $\frac{2}{3}$ **23** $\frac{4}{12}$ **24** $\frac{5}{9}$
25 $\frac{2}{4}$ **26** $\frac{5}{7}$ **27** $\frac{6}{12}$ **28** $\frac{3}{10}$ **29** $\frac{1}{8}$ **30** $\frac{4}{11}$

46

1 £6 **2** £12 **3** £9 **4** £57
5 £20 **6** £10 **7** 43 **8** 2
9 1 **10** 74 **11** 7 **12** 26
13 9 m **14** 16 m **15** 3 m **16** 89 m
17 31 m **18** 3 m **19** 0·3 **20** 9·78
21 6·4 **22** 1·05 **23** 3·2 **24** 2·5

25
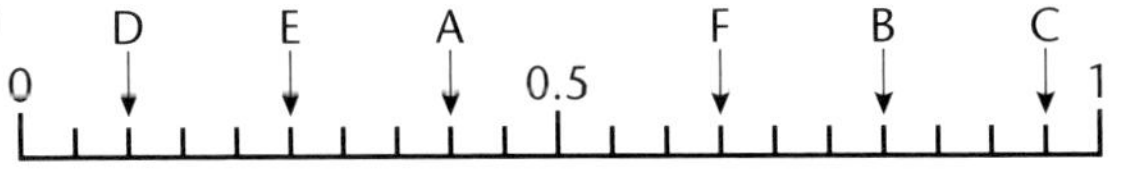

26 3·7 3·77 7 7·07 7·3
27 0·66 5·56 5·6 6·06 6·5
28 1·99 9·1 9·19 9·9 11·1
29 0·44 2·24 2·4 4·02 4·2
30 0·8 8·08 8·8 8·88 80·8

47

1 4·4 cm, 3·0 cm, 14·8 cm
2 3·5 cm, 2·4 cm, 11·8 cm
3 14 cm
4 26 cm
5 30 cm

6

Length	Width	Perimeter
6 cm	1·2 cm	14·4 cm
12 cm	10 cm	44 cm
5 m	4·5 m	19 m
7·5 m	6 m	27 m
2·8 cm	1·6 cm	8·8 cm
4·3 cm	2·5 cm	13·6 cm

7 *x* 10 cm *y* 10 cm Perimeter 52 cm
8 *x* 5 cm *y* 4 cm Perimeter 38 cm

48

1 38 cm **2** 81 cm **3** 550 g **4** 70 g **5** 190 ml **6** 720 ml **7** 660 m **8** 430 m
9 4·5 m **10** 2·4 m **11** 1·4 kg **12** 2·4 kg **13** 400 ml **14** 70 ml **15** 900 m **16** 80 m
17 250 ml **18** 10 ml **19** 580 m **20** 340 m **21** 65 cm **22** 13 cm **23** 290 g **24** 420 g
25 3 litres **26** 4·2 litres **27** 1·8 km **28** 6·4 km **29** 50 cm **30** 6 cm **31** 700 g **32** 80 g

50

1 rectangle
2 rhombus
3 parallelogram
4 square

51

1 (3, 2) (5, 5) (5, 2)
2 (1, 1) (1, 4) (3, 4) (3, 1)
3 (0, 6) (2, 6) (3, 4)
4 (3, 1) (3, 4) (5, 4) (5, 3) (4, 3) (4, 1)
5 (4, 4) (6, 5) (6, 2)
6 (1, 3) (4, 3) (3, 2) (3, 1) (2, 1) (2, 2)

52

1 5142 **2** 8020 **3** 6185 **4** 1458 **5** 3649
6 565 **7** 6652 **8** 4123 **9** 7472 **10** 3547
11 754 **12** 2579 **13** 7251 **14** 8362 **15** 5064
16 3167 **17** 5961 **18** 4305

53

1 2784 **2** 1158 **3** 6525 **4** 4202 **5** 2072 **6** 1941
7 2910 **8** 1870 **9** 4552 **10** 3024 **11** 4347 **12** 6444
13 65 **14** 37 **15** 86 **16** 38 **17** 59 **18** 96
19 38 **20** 27 **21** 84 **22** 95 **23** 47 **24** 57

54

1 180 **2** 75 **3** 240 **4** 150
5 72 **6** 9 **7** 70 **8** 28
9 2 **10** $1\frac{1}{2}$ **11** 3 **12** $\frac{1}{2}$
13 4 **14** $2\frac{1}{2}$ **15** 5 **16** 3
17 15 **18** 35 **19** 25 **20** 55
21 2 **22** 20 **23** 11 **24** 15
25 June 9th **26** August 28th
27 January 31st **28** December 6th

55

1 40 **2** 7:08 **3** 3:36
4 17 **5** 2:28 **6** 5:12
7 10:23 **8** 58 **9** 5:36
10 7:38 **11** 4:20 **12** 32

56

1 a) white **b)** green
2 a) lilac **b)** pink
3 a) 14 **b)** 11
4 7
5 7
6 71
7 a) £400 **b)** £650
8 a) Saturday **b)** Tuesday **c)** Friday **d)** Thursday
9 £300
10 £150
11 a) £1600 **b)** £3200

57

1 a) 28°C **b)** 7°C
2 a) Feb **b)** June
3 25°C
4 6°C

5 a) March–April
b) October–November
6 a) 200
b) 650
7 a) £501–£1000
b) £2001–£2500
8 a) 550 **b)** 550
9 50
10 250
11 50
12 2350

58

1 99
2 143
3 28, 91
4 48, 84
5 4, 5, 6
6 8, 9, 10
7 19, 20, 21
8 36, 37, 38
9 4, 5
10 6, 7
11 10, 11
12 7, 8
13 4
14 12
15 24
16 46
17 5
18 27
19 8
20 60

59

1 7 mm
2 21 mm
3 £10
4 £30
5 6 m
6 42 m
7 50 ml
8 450 ml
9 4 kg
10 8 kg
11 9p
12 36p
13 42 cm
14 9 kg
15 10p
16 10 mm
17 25 g
18 £24
19 15p
20 8 km
21 60 g
22 70 cm
23 8 kg
24 £50
25 30 g
26 44 cm
27 12p
28 36 m
29 £20
30 900 ml

60

1 five thousand and ninety-two
2 two thousand seven hundred and eight
3 3344 3433 3434 4333
4 6680 6688 6808 6886
5 50
6 800
7 2000
8 30
9 2801
10 4826
11 5742
12 7997
13 5700 6000
14 3300 3000
15 1500 2000
16 9700 10 000
17 XXXV
18 XLIX
19 LXXII
20 XCVI
21 69
22 27
23 84
24 58
25 63
26 8138
27 80
28 1550
29 −3
30 −2
31 −5
32 −6

61

1 130
2 700
3 6212
4 63
5 2407
6 450
7 123
8 85
9 174
10 77
11 2400
12 90
13 0
14 700
15 720
16 2000
17 90
18 1210
19 1200
20 420
21 9220
22 1162
23 6732
24 69
25 5544
26 2844
27 1985
28 54
29 8013
30 4596
31 4836
32 38

62

1 $\frac{2}{8}$
2 $\frac{3}{9}$
3 $\frac{10}{12}$
4 $\frac{5}{10}$
5 $\frac{9}{12}$
6 $\frac{4}{6}$
7 $\frac{8}{10}$
8 $\frac{4}{8}$
9 $\frac{5}{8}$
10 $\frac{3}{5}$
11 $\frac{11}{12}$
12 $\frac{2}{6}$
13 $\frac{1}{3}$
14 $\frac{4}{10}$
15 12
16 14
17 45
18 60
19 35
20 60
21 0·27
22 0·5
23 0·6
24 0·09
25 0·75
26 0·63
27 3·6
28 0·7
29 2
30 8·5
31 0·53
32 0·9
33 0·04
34 0·68
35 2
36 $\frac{9}{100}$
37 $\frac{4}{10}$
38 90
39 $\frac{2}{100}$
40 $\frac{6}{10}$
41 7
42 $\frac{8}{100}$
43 4
44 28
45 37
46 14
47 72
48 19
49 81
50 8

63

1 2·8
2 0·09
3 4·65
4 0·5
5 0·14
6 3·2
7 0·08
8 1·75
9 3
10 180
11 57
12 1240
13 600
14 2130
15 5900
16 420
17 28 cm^2, 22 cm
18 144 cm^2, 48 cm
19 12 cm, 4 cm, 40 cm
20 6 cm, 10 cm, 50 cm

21

12-Hour	7:35 am	1:19 pm	2:43 am	6:27 pm	5:51 am	11:04 pm
24-Hour	07:35	13:19	02:43	18:27	05:51	23:04

64

1 DABC
2 FHGE
3 G
4 ADFH
5 BCE
11 rectangle
12 trapezium

65

1 133
2 300 cm^2
3 7
4 −3
5 0·09
6 67
7 350 ml
8 7040
9 54
10 0·24
11 3235
12 40
13 5
14 400
15 XLIX
16 $\frac{6}{10}$
17 $\frac{3}{10}$
18 2·7 kg
19 132
20 2100
21 76
22 550

YEAR 5 PRACTICE WORKBOOK ANSWERS

1

1 300
2 7000
3 80
4 90 000
5 500 000
6 4
7 600
8 2 000 000
9 4000
10 60
11 3 000 000
12 200 000
13 800
14 50 000
15 8000
16 700 000
17 217 883
18 50 029
19 3 085 352
20 6 435 974
21 2 052 806
22 433 240
23 1 720 018
24 2 379 161
25 405 427
26 1 364 695

27 1839 1893 1938 1983
28 23 464 24 336 24 343 26 334
29 155 177 155 717 157 157 157 175
30 8282 20 808 22 008 22 028

2

1 48
2 27
3 36
4 99
5 12
6 5
7 10
8 7
9 9
10 7
11 12
12 6
13 24
14 5
15 56
16 108
17 6
18 8
19 12
20 6
21 11
22 7
23 8
24 9

25

×	9	4	12	10	6	3	8	5	11	7
2	18	8	24	20	12	6	16	10	22	14
8	72	32	96	80	48	24	64	40	88	56
5	45	20	60	50	30	15	40	25	55	35
3	27	12	36	30	18	9	24	15	33	21
11	99	44	132	110	66	33	88	55	121	77
7	63	28	84	70	42	21	56	35	77	49
4	36	16	48	40	24	12	32	20	44	28
12	108	48	144	120	72	36	96	60	132	84
6	54	24	72	60	36	18	48	30	66	42
9	81	36	108	90	54	27	72	45	99	63

3

1 3 6 9 12 15 18 21 24
2 8 16 24 32 40 48 56 64
3 21 42 63 84 105 126 147 168
4 40 80 120 160 200 240 280 320
5 25 50 75 100 125 150 175 200
6 109 218 327 436 545 654 763 872
7 Yes
8 Yes
9 No
10 Yes
11 Yes
12 No
13 Yes
14 Yes
15 No
16 Yes
17 No
18 No
19 No
20 Yes
21 Yes
22 No
23 37, 52
24 51, 102
25 82, 124
26 27, 78
27 56
28 65
29 187
30 396

4

1 1, 2, 5, 10, 25, 50
2 1, 2, 3, 6, 9, 18
3 1, 2, 3, 4, 6, 8, 12, 16, 24, 48
4 1, 2, 4, 7, 14, 28
5 1, 3, 9, 11, 33, 99
6 1, 2, 3, 4, 5, 6, 10, 12, 15, 20, 30, 60
7 1, 2, 4, 13, 26, 52
8 1, 3, 7, 9, 21, 63
9 1, 11, 121
10 1, 3, 5, 9, 15, 27, 45, 135
11 1, 2, 4, 37, 74, 148
12 1, 2, 3, 4, 6, 8, 9, 12, 18, 24, 36, 72
13 3
14 5
15 2, 4, 8
16 2
17 2, 4
18 5, 25
19 2, 4, 5, 10, 20
20 2, 4, 8

5

1 $\frac{4}{8}$
2 $\frac{6}{9}$
3 $\frac{6}{10}$
4 $\frac{10}{12}$
5 $\frac{4}{12}$
6 $\frac{2}{4}$
7 $\frac{8}{12}$
8 $\frac{6}{8}$
9 $\frac{6}{12}$
10 $\frac{8}{10}$
11 $\frac{4}{6}$
12 $\frac{30}{100}$
13 $\frac{3}{12}$
14 $\frac{5}{10}$
15 $\frac{4}{12}$
16 $\frac{3}{9}$
17 $\frac{4}{10}$
18 $\frac{70}{100}$
19 $\frac{4}{8}$
20 $\frac{9}{12}$
21 $\frac{12}{20}$
22 $\frac{4}{12}$
23 $\frac{15}{20}$
24 $\frac{3}{6}$
25 $\frac{5}{20}$
26 $\frac{8}{12}$
27 $\frac{10}{25}$
28 $\frac{8}{12}$

6

1 87
2 101
3 140
4 124
5 152
6 38
7 45
8 69
9 83
10 28
11 1630
12 15 500
13 114 000
14 13 300
15 1 200 000
16 630
17 4500
18 57 000
19 890
20 7800
21 142 748
22 1 441 319
23 20 326
24 100 573
25 1 571 860
26 430 035
27 168 991
28 2 425 607
29 638 152
30 1 864 384
31 461 097
32 417 762
33 5 130 310
34 422 965
35 2 364 202
36 636 047
37 2 659 728
38 865 859
39 736 684
40 7 800 496

7

1 42 331
2 58 411
3 41 864
4 59 805
5 94 194
6 86 790
7 70 392
8 59 026
9 82 214
10 101 305
11 90 734
12 56 940
13 106 032
14 144 520
15 133 505
16 64 010
17 75 030
18 122 503

8

1 9867
2 21 442
3 9843
4 44 357
5 36 527
6 23 530
7 20 387
8 24 863
9 75 617
10 12 755
11 59 758
12 53 673
13 24 709
14 69 572
15 6057
16 49 918
17 36 942
18 7502

9

allow +/− 5° for angle size

1 *a* acute 75°
b obtuse 95°
c reflex 280°
d obtuse 110°
order *a b d c*

2 *e* acute 70°
f obtuse 95°
g acute 85°
h obtuse 110°
order *e g f h*

3 *i* reflex 200°
j obtuse 155°
k acute 30°
l reflex 315°
order *k j i l*

4 *m* acute 40°
n obtuse 125°
o acute 60°
p obtuse 135°
order *m o n p*

10

1 30°
2 160°
3 75°
4 115°
5 60°
6 145°
7 15°
8 100°
9 50°
10 140°
11 95°
12 5°
13 135°
14 20°
15 105°
16 65°
17 55° acute
18 230° reflex
19 110° obtuse
20 *a* 75°
b 115°
c 105°
d 65°

11

1 23 000
2 19
3 740 000
4 6800
5 3500
6 271
7 9200
8 4830
9 70 000
10 35 090
11 18 000
12 620
13 514 000
14 80
15 360 000
16 20
17 1000
18 10
19 100
20 1000
21 10
22 100
23 1000
24 1000
25 10
26 100
27 100
28 10
29 100
30 100
31 100
32 1000

12

1 $5\frac{3}{7}$
2 $6\frac{1}{3}$
3 $9\frac{5}{6}$
4 $8\frac{11}{12}$
5 $4\frac{2}{9}$
6 $24\frac{3}{5}$
7 $7\frac{4}{11}$
8 $75\frac{1}{2}$
9 $6\frac{5}{8}$
10 $26\frac{9}{10}$
11 $9\frac{5}{7}$
12 $31\frac{3}{4}$
13 $12\frac{7}{9}$
14 $21\frac{2}{3}$
15 $3\frac{77}{100}$
16 $7\frac{1}{6}$
17 8·75
18 15·6
19 9.4
20 2·25
21 46·5
22 13·64
23 3·5
24 5·5
25 £4·60
26 £64·50
27 £16·80
28 £11·50
29 £8·40
30 £14·25
31 £27·20
32 £53·50

13

1 0·26
2 4·7
3 0·925
4 1·08
5 0·009
6 0·3
7 7·12
8 2·354
9 0·09
10 0·067
11 19·6
12 1·406
13 $9\frac{3}{10}$
14 $\frac{625}{1000}$
15 $\frac{96}{100}$
16 $2\frac{137}{1000}$
17 $\frac{82}{1000}$
18 $18\frac{4}{10}$
19 $\frac{3}{1000}$
20 $5\frac{29}{100}$
21 $\frac{708}{1000}$
22 $1\frac{11}{1000}$
23 $3\frac{8}{10}$
24 $6\frac{6}{1000}$
25 $\frac{7}{10}$
26 $\frac{8}{100}$
27 $\frac{4}{1000}$
28 3
29 $\frac{8}{10}$
30 $\frac{9}{100}$
31 $\frac{5}{1000}$
32 $\frac{6}{10}$
33 $\frac{9}{1000}$
34 $\frac{6}{100}$
35 $\frac{2}{10}$
36 $\frac{6}{1000}$

14

1 0·13
2 0·66
3 0·28
4 0·92
5 0·49
6 0·85
7 0·37
8 0·71
9 0·54
10 0·06
11 2·3
12 5·7
13 0·9
14 8·2
15 3·6
16 9·8
17 1·4
18 7·5
19 4·1
20 6·7
21 1·34
22 2·22
23 8·09
24 3·45
25 10·208
26 5·53
27 2·809
28 5·44
29 8·08
30 3·92
31 4·155
32 9·66
33 4·083
34 8·777
35 2·402
36 9·14
37 1·35
38 2·832
39 6·01
40 7·26

15

1 2·8
2 4
3 8·32
4 0·57
5 690
6 6
7 0·07
8 1520
9 0·68
10 5·3
11 2130
12 90
13 1·05
14 0·06
15 240
16 900
17 32·5
18 19
19 0·2
20 14·7
21 54
22 518
23 0·64
24 2900
25 1·2
26 0·06
27 700
28 3850
29 0·31
30 9·18
31 4500
32 30

16

1 8.4 km
2 25
3 5.11 m
4 200
5 1.76 km
6 2.3 kg
7 10.5 m
8 19.5 kg

17

1 −3°C
2 8th
3 −2°C
4 11th
5 3°C
6 5°C
7 **a)** 3rd, 4th **b)** 7th, 8th
8 **a)** 4th–5th **b)** 11th–12th
9 15
10 April
11 July
12 £95
13 September and October
14 May and June
15 15
16 10
17 5
18 555

18

1 acute
2 obtuse
3 obtuse
4 acute
5 obtuse
6 acute
7 C 75° (allow +/− 1°)
8 G 85° (allow +/− 1°)

19

1 9
2 7
3 3
4 5
5 6
6 2
7 4
8 7
9 5
10 8
11 3
12 6
13 50
14 100
15 11
16 $4\frac{1}{3}$
17 $8\frac{2}{3}$
18 $5\frac{2}{3}$
19 $11\frac{1}{3}$
20 $7\frac{6}{10}$
21 $3\frac{9}{10}$
22 $6\frac{2}{10}$
23 $12\frac{5}{10}$
24 $2\frac{3}{8}$
25 $5\frac{1}{8}$
26 $9\frac{4}{8}$
27 $3\frac{6}{8}$
28 $3\frac{3}{4}$
29 $11\frac{1}{2}$
30 $2\frac{8}{12}$
31 $5\frac{2}{5}$
32 $8\frac{5}{11}$
33 $1\frac{3}{7}$
34 $2\frac{35}{100}$
35 $7\frac{7}{9}$
36 $9\frac{2}{3}$
37 $4\frac{3}{10}$
38 $12\frac{5}{6}$
39 $6\frac{2}{8}$

20

1 120
2 10
3 180
4 5
5 48
6 5
7 28
8 12
9 24
10 7
11 100
12 5 mins 30 secs
13 135
14 8 hours 20 mins
15 34
16 4 days 4 hours
17 17
18 5 weeks 5 days
19 44
20 5 years 3 months
21 1800
22 720
23 **a)** 8 w 4 d **b)** 13 w 1 d
24 **a)** Tuesday **b)** Saturday

21

8 25 prime numbers
2, 3, 5, 7, 11, 13, 17, 19, 23, 29, 31, 37, 41, 43, 47, 53, 59, 61, 67, 71, 73, 79, 83, 89, 97

22

1 5472
2 43 336
3 16 840
4 53 473
5 38 574
6 21 036
7 17 934
8 43 908
9 20 744
10 46 024
11 29 925
12 23 320
13 31 671
14 60 576
15 20 385
16 27 762
17 9875
18 62 896
19 44 856
20 21 725
21 24 606
22 39 468
23 44 304
24 39 294

23

1 67
2 43 r 2
3 59
4 75 r 5
5 124
6 138
7 222 r 3
8 148
9 136
10 274 r 1
11 387 r 2
12 158
13 129 r 3
14 357
15 138 r 9
16 149
17 175
18 146 r 4

24

1 $\frac{2}{3}$
2 $\frac{5}{8}$
3 $\frac{2}{3}$
4 $\frac{7}{8}$
5 $\frac{4}{5}$
6 $\frac{9}{10}$
7 $\frac{4}{5}$
8 $\frac{3}{4}$
9 $\frac{7}{10}$
10 $\frac{4}{9}$
11 $\frac{11}{12}$
12 $\frac{9}{10}$
13 $\frac{1}{4}$
14 $\frac{1}{2}$
15 $\frac{3}{4}$
16 $\frac{2}{3}$
17 $\frac{3}{12}$ $\frac{3}{10}$ $\frac{3}{5}$ $\frac{3}{4}$
18 $\frac{1}{3}$ $\frac{1}{2}$ $\frac{3}{5}$ $\frac{3}{4}$
19 $\frac{2}{7}$ $\frac{2}{5}$ $\frac{5}{9}$ $\frac{2}{3}$
20 $\frac{3}{8}$ $\frac{1}{2}$ $\frac{5}{8}$ $\frac{3}{4}$

25

1 $2\frac{1}{2}$
2 $5\frac{2}{3}$
3 $3\frac{1}{5}$
4 $1\frac{9}{11}$
5 $2\frac{5}{8}$
6 $1\frac{75}{100}$
7 $4\frac{9}{10}$
8 $1\frac{3}{7}$
9 $3\frac{5}{6}$
10 $2\frac{1}{3}$
11 $1\frac{7}{9}$
12 $2\frac{7}{12}$
13 $2\frac{1}{4}$
14 $4\frac{3}{8}$
15 $2\frac{2}{5}$
16 $5\frac{1}{100}$
17 $\frac{7}{4}$
18 $\frac{13}{6}$
19 $\frac{86}{10}$
20 $\frac{17}{12}$
21 $\frac{9}{2}$
22 $\frac{15}{8}$
23 $\frac{31}{9}$
24 $\frac{5}{3}$
25 $\frac{22}{7}$
26 $\frac{9}{5}$
27 $\frac{244}{100}$
28 $\frac{13}{4}$
29 $\frac{17}{10}$
30 $\frac{59}{12}$
31 $\frac{35}{11}$

26

1 40 **3** 40 minutes **5** 1600 **7** £720
2 270 **4** 36 **6** 35 **8** 80

27

1 240	**10** 280 000	**19** 8300	**28** 660 000
2 5060	**11** 127 000	**20** 13 000	**29** 390 000
3 71 320	**12** 930 000	**21** 5700	**30** 830 000
4 94 680	**13** 500 000	**22** 290 300	**31** 1 000 000
5 308 580	**14** 1 800 000	**23** 76 000	**32** 1 000 000
6 412 750	**15** 9 000 000	**24** 185 000	**33** 4 000 000
7 17 000	**16** 3 900 000	**25** 260 000	**34** 4 000 000
8 505 000	**17** 8 200 000	**26** 60 000	**35** 7 000 000
9 82 000	**18** 5 300 000	**27** 200 000	**36** 2 000 000

28

1 A −15°C B −7°C C −2°C D 7°C E 14°C

2 9°C	**10** −3°C	**18** −13°C
3 21°C	**11** 3°C	**19** −6°C
4 13°C	**12** 5°C	**20** … −2 0 2 4
5 16°C	**13** −5°C	**21** … 1 0 −1 −2
6 14°C	**14** −10°C	**22** −7 −5 −3 −1 …
7 29°C	**15** −13°C	**23** −15 −10 −5 0 …
8 2°C	**16** −1°C	
9 6°C	**17** −7°C	

29

1 41 153	**5** 43 278	**9** 94 828	**13** 82 472	**17** 67 201
2 62 634	**6** 15 833	**10** 44 744	**14** 54 034	**18** 6846
3 78 360	**7** 67 023	**11** 27 042	**15** 72 305	
4 14 576	**8** 40 134	**12** 21 977	**16** 37 547	

30

1 *a* 55°	**7** *g* 140°	**13** *m* 110°	*n* 70°
2 *b* 132°	**8** *h* 315°	**14** *o* 145°	*p* 35°
3 *c* 81°	**9** *i* 168°	**15** *q* 128°	*r* 52°
4 *d* 150°	**10** *j* 244°	**16** *s* 93°	*t* 87°
5 *e* 104°	**11** *k* 83°	**17** *u* 139°	*v* 41°
6 *f* 67°	**12** *l* 211°	**18** *w* 116°	*x* 64°

31

allow +/− 0·1 cm

1 *a* 105° *b* 3·9 cm **3** *f* 135° *g* 45°
2 *c* 4·1 cm *d* 3·0 cm *e* 130° **4** *h* 55° *i* 125°

32

1

LENGTH	WIDTH	PERIMETER	AREA
7 cm	4 cm	22 cm	28 cm^2
15 cm	3 cm	36 cm	45 cm^2
8 cm	8 cm	32 cm	64 cm^2
9 cm	7 cm	32 cm	63 cm^2
10 cm	2 cm	24 cm	20 cm^2
16 cm	3 cm	38 cm	48 cm^2
40 cm	20 cm	120 cm	800 cm^2
12 cm	12 cm	48 cm	144 cm^2
20 cm	5 cm	50 cm	100 cm^2

2 *w*	= 7 cm	A	= 42 cm^2
x	= 3 cm	B	= 9 cm^2
Perim.	= 32 cm	Total	= 51 cm^2
3 *y*	= 25 cm	C	= 375 cm^2
z	= 5 cm	D	= 75 cm^2
Perim.	= 90 cm	Total	= 450 cm^2

33

1 3995	**5** 7738	**9** 92 304	**13** 63 936
2 4350	**6** 35 252	**10** 279 864	**14** 152 964
3 24 102	**7** 58 048	**11** 48 203	**15** 94 068
4 35 112	**8** 159 970	**12** 166 275	

34

1 27	**4** 69 678	**7** 6875
2 52 270	**5** 185	**8** £29 940
3 768	**6** £46 305	**9** 716

35

1 a) 1·4	**b)** 1·4	**9 a)** £9	**b)** £8·60	**17** $<$
2 a) 3·76	**b)** 3·8	**10 a)** £15	**b)** £15·10	**18** $>$
3 a) 17·44	**b)** 17·4	**11 a)** £8	**b)** £7·90	**19** $>$
4 a) 0·93	**b)** 0·9	**12 a)** £24	**b)** £24·30	**20** $<$
5 a) 26·25	**b)** 26·3	**13 a)** £10	**b)** £9·90	**21** $>$
6 a) 9·85	**b)** 9·8	**14 a)** £1	**b)** £0·60	**22** $<$
7 a) 62·57	**b)** 62·6	**15 a)** £3	**b)** £3·50	**23** $>$
8 a) 4·98	**b)** 5·0	**16 a)** £19	**b)** £18·70	**24** $<$

25 0·272 0·277 0·72 0·722 **27** 9·33 9·34 9·403 9·43
26 0·005 0·055 0·505 0·55 **28** 0·116 0·16 0·166 0·6

36

1 $\frac{5}{8}$ $\frac{6}{8}$ $\frac{7}{8}$ 1 $1\frac{1}{8}$ $1\frac{2}{8}$ **7** 0.1 0.3 0.5 0.7 0.9 1.1
2 5 $4\frac{1}{2}$ 4 $3\frac{1}{2}$ 3 $2\frac{1}{2}$ **8** 3.7 3.2 2.7 2.2 1.7 1.2
3 0 $\frac{2}{5}$ $\frac{4}{5}$ $1\frac{1}{5}$ $1\frac{3}{5}$ 2 **9** 0 0.4 0.8 1.2 1.6 2.0
4 $2\frac{3}{6}$ $2\frac{2}{6}$ $2\frac{1}{6}$ 2 $1\frac{5}{6}$ $1\frac{4}{6}$ **10** 10 9.1 8.2 7.3 6.4 5.5
5 1 $1\frac{2}{3}$ $2\frac{1}{3}$ 3 $3\frac{2}{3}$ $4\frac{1}{3}$ **11** 1.0 1.8 2.6 3.4 4.2 5.0
6 $4\frac{1}{2}$ $3\frac{3}{4}$ 3 $2\frac{1}{4}$ $1\frac{1}{2}$ $\frac{3}{4}$ **12** 3.0 2.7 2.4 2.1 1.8 1.5

13 0.25 0.5 0.75 1.0 1.25 1.5 1.75 2.0 2.25 2.5
14 0.1 0.25 0.4 0.55 0.7 0.85 1.0 1.15 1.3 1.45
15 0.6 0.65 0.7 0.75 0.8 0.85 0.9 0.95 1.0 1.05
16 0.96 0.98 1.0 1.02 1.04 1.06 1.08 1.1 1.12 1.14

37

1 38 m	**9** 0·109 km	**17** 62 litres	**25** 0·003 litres
2 29 kg	**10** 0·4 kg	**18** 90 m	**26** 2·05 km
3 500 km	**11** 0·67 cm	**19** 3·75 kg	**27** 0·04 kg
4 170 litres	**12** 2·5 litres	**20** 840 km	**28** 6·18 cm
5 0·6 cm	**13** 3·9 m	**21** 113 litres	**29** 0·5 litres
6 46 kg	**14** 0·08 kg	**22** 0·08 cm	**30** 3·7 m
7 0·3 m	**15** 0·041 km	**23** 2·6 kg	**31** 0·099 kg
8 85·2 litres	**16** 0·007 litres	**24** 7900 m	**32** 0·406 km

38

1 May
2 September
3 peas
4 carrots and leeks
5 parsnips and leeks
6 parsnips and potatoes
7 beans
8 potatoes
9 carrots and leeks
10 October and November
11 potatoes
12 8

39

4 (3,1)	**5** (4,3)	**6** (1,4)
(2,3)	(5,5)	(3,5)
(6,3)	(6,3)	(4,3)
(5,1)	(5,1)	

40

1 175·039	**4** 145·32	**7** 6·579	**10** 122·036
2 41·425	**5** 202·13	**8** 37·49	**11** 48·083
3 21·856	**6** 65·261	**9** 134·305	**12** 59·243

41

1 36	**11** 8	**21** 30 000	**31** 900	**41** 9000
2 24	**12** 12	**22** 2800	**32** 50	**42** 1200
3 63	**13** 11	**23** 640	**33** 8400	**43** 700
4 56	**14** 3	**24** 24 000	**34** 1000	**44** 90
5 30	**15** 12	**25** 120	**35** 960	**45** 110
6 144	**16** 4	**26** 700	**36** 420 000	**46** 3000
7 0	**17** 140	**27** 1200	**37** 2400	**47** 800
8 48	**18** 5400	**28** 60	**38** 540	**48** 120
9 9	**19** 1210	**29** 80	**39** 48 000	
10 6	**20** 10 800	**30** 11 000	**40** 360	

42

1 26 480	**6** 49 638	**11** 25 865	**16** 736	**21** 158 r 2
2 9688	**7** 20 776	**12** 76 644	**17** 126 r 3	**22** 487
3 33 822	**8** 55 924	**13** 183	**18** 154 r 4	**23** 209 r 3
4 11 538	**9** 29 024	**14** 279 r 2	**19** 265 r 3	**24** 149 r 6
5 23 340	**10** 41 661	**15** 147 r 9	**20** 173	

43

1 $\frac{9}{10}$	**5** $1\frac{4}{8}$	**9** $\frac{4}{10}$	**13** $\frac{8}{12}$	**17** $\frac{2}{6}$
2 $\frac{5}{7}$	**6** $\frac{3}{9}$	**10** $\frac{2}{6}$	**14** $1\frac{1}{10}$	**18** $\frac{8}{10}$
3 $1\frac{1}{3}$	**7** $\frac{6}{12}$	**11** $\frac{7}{10}$	**15** $1\frac{3}{12}$	**19** $\frac{7}{9}$
4 $1\frac{2}{5}$	**8** $\frac{2}{4}$	**12** $\frac{3}{6}$	**16** $\frac{3}{8}$	**20** $\frac{7}{12}$

44

1 27	**5** 40	**9** 100	**13** 84	**17** 39
2 8	**6** 30	**10** 24	**14** 20	**18** 2590
3 72	**7** 21	**11** 44	**15** 56	**19** 95
4 25	**8** 21	**12** 400	**16** 315	**20** 88

45

1 157, 243 **2** 106, 144 **3** 448 **4** 765

5 $\begin{array}{r} 3\ 8\ 5 \\ +\ 1\ 6\ 9 \\ \hline \end{array}$ **6** $\begin{array}{r} 6\ 3\ 8 \\ -\ 2\ 7\ 4 \\ \hline \end{array}$ **7** $\begin{array}{r} 8\ 2\ 0 \\ -\ 5\ 3\ 5 \\ \hline \end{array}$

8

14	7	11	2
1	12	8	13
4	9	5	16
15	6	10	3

9

19	10	14	7
8	13	9	20
5	16	12	17
18	11	15	6

10

13	8	18	11
10	19	5	16
7	14	12	17
20	9	15	6

11 88, 89 **12** 58, 59, 60

46

1 *a* 10	*b* 5	**5** *a* 25°	*b* 40°	*c* 65°
2 *c* 12	*d* 25	**6** *d* 48°	*e* 84°	*f* 96°
3 *e* 8	*f* 9	**7** *g* 19°	*h* 55°	*i* 74°
4 *g* 8	*h* 24	**8** *j* 51°	*k* 34°	*l* 73°
		m 107°	*n* 141°	

47

1 (1, 3) (2, 6) (4, 6) (3, 3)
2 (3, 0) (3, 2) (5, 2) (5, 4) (6, 4) (6, 0)
3 (2, 2) (6, 2) (4, 0)
4 (0, 0) (0, 2) (2, 4) (2, 2)
5 (1, 6) (6, 6) (5, 4) (2, 4)
6 (4, 3) (5, 5) (6, 4) (6, 2) (5, 1)

48

1 (1, 0) (2, 2) (3, 0)
2 (1, 3) (2, 4) (3, 4) (4, 3)
3 (0, 3) (0, 5) (1, 5) (2, 4) (1, 3)
4 (5, 1) (4, 4) (6, 3)
5 (1, 1) (2, 3) (5, 3) (4, 1)
6 (3, 4) (3, 5) (4, 5) (5, 4) (5, 3) (4, 3)

49

1 74	**11** 252	**21** CLXXIII	**31** DCCXVIII
2 398	**12** 807	**22** DXLV	**32** CMLXV
3 725	**13** 934	**23** CMXXVII	**33** CXCVII
4 462	**14** 119	**24** CCCLXXXII	**34** DLI
5 837	**15** 593	**25** DCCIV	**35** CCLXXVI
6 281	**16** 368	**26** CDLVIII	**36** DCCCXXIV
7 956	**17** 420	**27** XCI	**37** CDXXXIII
8 609	**18** 746	**28** DCCCLXIX	**38** CCCXCIX
9 143	**19** 685	**29** CCXXXVI	**39** CMXLII
10 514	**20** 979	**30** DCX	**40** DCLXXXIX

50

1 16	**7** 27	**13** 2500	**19** 157	**25** 6	**31** 120
2 49	**8** 1000	**14** 6400	**20** 140	**26** 3	**32** 90
3 121	**9** 400	**15** 1	**21** 16 200	**27** 10	**33** 5
4 81	**10** 900	**16** 343	**22** 700	**28** 8	**34** 8
5 144	**11** 3600	**17** 89	**23** 729	**29** 70	**35** 4
6 25	**12** 10 000	**18** 19	**24** 216	**30** 50	**36** 20

37 a) 1000 **b)** 100

51

1 inches	**9** <	**17** >	**25** 10 kg
2 miles	**10** >	**18** <	**26** 450 cm
3 feet	**11** <	**19** >	**27** 300 ml
4 yards	**12** >	**20** >	**28** 3 m
5 pounds	**13** <	**21** 90 g	**29** 150 g
6 ounces	**14** <	**22** 16 km	**30** 3 km (allow 3·2 km)
7 pints	**15** >	**23** 9 litres	**31** 225 litres
8 gallons	**16** <	**24** 20 cm	**32** 30 cm

52

1 perimeter of flat	36 m
perimeter of lounge	30 m
area of flat	80 m^2
area of kitchen	12 m^2
area of bedroom	24 m^2
area of lounge	44 m^2
2 perimeter of building	172 m
perimeter of office	60 m
area of building	1800 m^2
area of shop	1080 m^2
area of office	200 m^2
area of stockroom	520 m^2

3 21 m

53

1 $\frac{7}{10}$ $\frac{8}{10}$ $\frac{9}{10}$ 1 $1\frac{1}{10}$ $1\frac{2}{10}$
2 $1\frac{2}{5}$ $1\frac{1}{5}$ 1 $\frac{4}{5}$ $\frac{3}{5}$ $\frac{2}{5}$
3 $\frac{2}{8}$ $\frac{4}{8}$ $\frac{6}{8}$ 1 $1\frac{2}{8}$ $1\frac{4}{8}$
4 $3\frac{3}{4}$ 3 $2\frac{1}{4}$ $1\frac{1}{2}$ $\frac{3}{4}$ 0
5 $-\frac{2}{3}$ $-\frac{1}{3}$ 0 $\frac{1}{3}$ $\frac{2}{3}$ 1
6 3·8 3·6 3·4 3·2 3 2·8
7 2·8 3·3 3·8 4·3 4·8 5·3
8 9·1 8·2 7·3 6·4 5·5 4·6
9 −0·6 −0·2 0·2 0·6 1 1·4
10 0·3 0·2 0·1 0 −0·1 −0·2
11 $1\frac{2}{6}$
12 $5\frac{3}{4}$
13 $1\frac{5}{10}$
14 $-3\frac{2}{5}$
15 $5\frac{1}{2}$
16 1·2
17 3·4
18 1·2
19 0·5
20 −0·3

54

1 12:42
2 27
3 2
4 56
5 15:05
6 3
7 11:09
8 2 hours 47 minutes
9 27
10 07:52
11 14:02
12 3 hours 38 minutes

55

1 27 873
2 23 045
3 21 108
4 49 542
5 12 768
6 11 860
7 27 104
8 43 560
9 16 428
10 17 244
11 51 432
12 56 556
13 456r5
14 374
15 738
16 518r7
17 693r2
18 369r1
19 783
20 609r3
21 287r4
22 792
23 270r10
24 539r4

56

1 1323
2 £145
3 118
4 1152
5 92 084
6 120 miles

57

1 68
2 12
3 132
4 37
5 13
6 189
7 49
8 83
9 62
10 9
11 180
12 55
13 5 and 6
14 8 and 9
15 13 and 14
16 19 and 20

58

1 68
2 21
3 83
4 6
5 420
6 770
7 150
8 390
9 540
10 980
11 0·65
12 0·09
13 0·72
14 0·18
15 0·44
16 0·37
17 0·95
18 0·53
19 0·86
20 0·61
21 32
22 5·4
23 33
24 18
25 56
26 40
27 120
28 50
29 90
30 70
31 9
32 120 g
33 3
34 110
35 20
36 3·6
37 14
38 48
39 6·3
40 55

59

1 45p
2 2·2 m
3 1·52 kg
4 1·52 litres
5 2·75 secs
6 280 dollars
7 235 m
8 1·2 kg
9 3·6 °C
10 400 ml
11 £4·28
12 160

60

1 30%
2 76%
3 25%
4 80%
5 9%
6 65%
7 83%
8 10%
9 27%
10 94%
11 60%
12 31%
13 a) $\frac{17}{100}$ b) 0·17
14 a) $\frac{2}{5}$ b) 0·4
15 a) $\frac{83}{100}$ b) 0·83
16 a) $\frac{1}{20}$ b) 0·05
17 a) $\frac{51}{100}$ b) 0·51
18 a) $\frac{1}{5}$ b) 0·2
19 a) $\frac{99}{100}$ b) 0·99
20 a) $\frac{3}{4}$ b) 0·75
21 a) $\frac{6}{25}$ b) 0·24
22 a) $\frac{9}{10}$ b) 0·9
23 a) $\frac{67}{100}$ b) 0·67
24 a) $\frac{1}{50}$ b) 0·02
25 25
26 14
27 150
28 48
29 90p
30 45p
31 72p
32 £6·25
33 480 m
34 7·5 cm
35 200 ml
36 480 g

61

1 30 000
2 80
3 5000
4 900
5 200 000
6 7000
7 40
8 10 000
9 $\frac{6}{10}$
10 $\frac{3}{1000}$
11 90 000
12 $\frac{5}{100}$
13 1155 1511 1515 1551
14 66 088 66 608 68 686 68 860
15 113 344 114 334 114 343 131 413
16 97 929 279 972 292 272 297 229
17 424 000
18 90 000
19 110 000
20 755 000
21 340 000
22 690 000
23 860 000
24 200 000
25 300 000
26 500 000
27 800 000
28 500 000
29 DCLXXXV
30 CCLXIV
31 CDXCII
32 DCCXXXVII
33 179
34 543
35 928
36 856

62

1 56 301
2 75 713
3 93 003
4 81 612
5 63 205
6 85 181
7 36 165
8 8636
9 32 484
10 59 668
11 35 288
12 33 925
13 17 724
14 33 714
15 53 466
16 32 395
17 19 152
18 23 712
19 357
20 163 r 7
21 179 r 1
22 182 r 6
23 175
24 148

63

1 $2\frac{1}{4}$
2 $1\frac{4}{7}$
3 $5\frac{2}{3}$
4 $1\frac{4}{11}$
5 $2\frac{59}{100}$
6 $3\frac{7}{8}$
7 $\frac{13}{2}$
8 $\frac{43}{10}$
9 $\frac{17}{6}$
10 $\frac{9}{5}$
11 $\frac{32}{9}$
12 $\frac{67}{12}$
13 $1\frac{2}{6}$
14 $1\frac{3}{8}$
15 $1\frac{3}{12}$
16 $\frac{5}{10}$
17 $\frac{8}{12}$
18 $\frac{3}{8}$
19 $\frac{8}{10}$
20 $\frac{5}{1000}$
21 9
22 $\frac{6}{100}$
23 $\frac{1}{100}$
24 $\frac{7}{1000}$
25 $\frac{2}{10}$
26 $\frac{3}{100}$
27 5
28 $\frac{4}{1000}$
29 $\frac{6}{10}$
30 $\frac{9}{1000}$

31

Fraction	Decimal	% age
$\frac{29}{100}$	0·29	29%
$\frac{1}{2}$	0·5	50%
$\frac{3}{100}$	0·03	3%
$\frac{7}{10}$	0·7	70%
$\frac{3}{4}$	0·75	75%
$\frac{41}{100}$	0·41	41%

32 $6\frac{1}{6}$
33 $4\frac{5}{12}$
34 $8\frac{2}{5}$
35 $3\frac{99}{100}$
36 24
37 10
38 15
39 54
40 1·8
41 3·5
42 60p
43 150 g

64

1 £0·19
2 £0·64
3 0·48
4 0·95
5 0·21
6 0·86
7 0·57
8 0·32
9 1·7 m
10 1625 km
11 23·8 kg
12 4090 litres
13 3·6 m
14 0·875 km
15 1·42 kg
16 0·029 litres
17 0·75 kg, 2·5 kg
18 0·3 m, 0·65 m
19 32 cm, 64 cm^2
20 90 cm, 500 cm^2
21 x 18 cm y 10 cm perimeter 66 cm area of A 180 cm^2 area of B 60 cm^2 total area 240 cm^2

65

1 6400
2 72
3 0·63
4 22·5 kg
5 20
6 700
7 0·2, 20%
8 270°
9 60
10 80 cm
11 255 555
12 CDLXXIX
13 $\frac{9}{10}$
14 6
15 80 cm
16 £6·51
17 27
18 440 ml
19 79 83 89 97
20 $\frac{31}{7}$

YEAR 6 PRACTICE WORKBOOK ANSWERS

1

1 700 000 **2** 900 **3** 30 000 **4** 5 000 000 **5** 80 **6** 6000 **7** 400 000
8 2 **9** 5000 **10** 10 000 **11** 60 **12** 2 000 000 **13** 400 **14** 900 000
15 30 **16** 80 000 **17** 2 043 918 **18** 710 264 **19** 300 040 **20** 980 000 **21** 4 984 032
22 6 497 175 **23** 1 001 829 **24** 8940 **25** 2 026 283 **26** 6 852 547

27 823 388 823 833 832 238 833 322
28 179 971 197 199 197 711 199 197
29 4 006 646 4 060 640 4 064 046 4 400 066
30 2 527 727 2 552 572 2 722 577 2 725 252

2

1 92 256 **2** 78 613 **3** 50 503 **4** 8349
5 40 546 **6** 58 748 **7** 87 012 **8** 41 063
9 75 830 **10** 27 658 **11** 11 649 **12** 24 674
13 64 338 **14** 100 024 **15** 76 722 **16** 49 692
17 81 693 **18** 6457

3

1 10 766 **2** 16 488 **3** 22 350 **4** 13 456 **5** 21 231
6 19 370 **7** 32 296 **8** 28 192 **9** 16 500 **10** 34 734
11 8508 **12** 33 534 **13** 85·11 **14** 591·6 **15** 1315·6
16 6514·8 **17** 147·8 **18** 206·14 **19** 3766·5 **20** 2454·9
21 210·76 **22** 383·52 **23** 1398·4 **24** 4579·2

4

1 2·513 **2** 0·79 **3** 0·428 **4** 7·105 **5** 5·06 **6** 0·039 **7** 9·874 **8** 1·35 **9** 0·006
10 3·082 **11** 0·04 **12** 8·697 **13** $6\frac{28}{100}$ **14** $\frac{517}{1000}$ **15** $1\frac{9}{10}$ **16** $4\frac{349}{1000}$ **17** $9\frac{6}{100}$ **18** $\frac{801}{1000}$
19 $3\frac{95}{1000}$ **20** $\frac{43}{100}$ **21** $\frac{2}{1000}$ **22** $2\frac{186}{1000}$ **23** $10\frac{1}{100}$ **24** $5\frac{703}{1000}$ **25** $\frac{4}{10}$ **26** $\frac{8}{1000}$ **27** 2
28 $\frac{5}{100}$ **29** $\frac{7}{10}$ **30** $\frac{9}{1000}$ **31** $\frac{3}{100}$ **32** 6 **33** $\frac{1}{10}$ **34** $\frac{2}{1000}$ **35** $\frac{8}{100}$ **36** $\frac{5}{10}$

5

1 42 **2** 103·6 **3** 5719 **4** 72·8 **5** 0·185 **6** 0·29 **7** 31·4
8 6·37 **9** 2·4 cm **10** 8·4 kg **11** 5·6 km **12** 3 litres **13** £0·72 **14** 0·18 m
15 0·3 kg **16** 0·36 litres **17** 13·16 **18** 410·2 **19** 44·55 **20** 139·2 **21** 14·8
22 322·2 **23** 4·11 **24** 159·0 **25** 96·6 **26** a) £13.50 b) £47.25 c) £81.00

6

1 *a* 35° **2** *b* 74° **3** *c* 70° **4** *d* 105° **5** *e* 61° **6** *f* 75°
7 *g* 122° **8** *h* 87° **9** *i* 42° **10** *j* 49° **11** *k* 25° **12** *l* 75°
13 120° **14** 135° **15** 108°

7

1 133° **2** 57° **3** 105° **4** 82° **5** 144° **6** 68°
7 50° **8** 266° **9** 123° **10** 282° **11** 205° **12** 81°
13 *m* 135° *n* 45°
14 *p* 67° *q* 113°
15 *r* 78° *s* 102°
16 *t* 121° *u* 59°
17 *v* 39° *w* 141°
18 *x* 86° *y* 94°

8

1 437 **2** 529 **3** 865 **4** 473 **5** 294 **6** 652
7 386 **8** 948 **9** 9·36 **10** 15·9 **11** 3·76 **12** 92·7
13 1·84 **14** 73·2 **15** 5·86 **16** 19·5 **17** 26·45 **18** 6·14
19 72·25 **20** 48·75 **21** 56·35 **22** 169·5 **23** 14·96 **24** 75·75

9

1 3·665 kg **2** 105 Euros **3** 2·11 seconds **4** 0·45 m **5** 8·685 litres **6** 4·32 kg **7** £16·75 **8** 379·04 km

10

1 $\frac{3}{6}$ **2** $\frac{8}{10}$ **3** $\frac{25}{100}$ **4** $\frac{14}{20}$ **5** $\frac{6}{9}$ **6** $\frac{2}{12}$ **7** $\frac{2}{4}$ **8** $\frac{30}{100}$
9 $\frac{6}{8}$ **10** $\frac{40}{100}$ **11** $\frac{4}{12}$ **12** $\frac{50}{100}$ **13** $\frac{10}{12}$ **14** $\frac{4}{16}$ **15** $\frac{10}{16}$ **16** $\frac{55}{100}$
17 $\frac{2}{3}$ **18** $\frac{9}{10}$ **19** $\frac{1}{5}$ **20** $\frac{3}{4}$ **21** $\frac{1}{2}$ **22** $\frac{1}{6}$ **23** $\frac{5}{8}$ **24** $\frac{2}{3}$
25 $\frac{3}{2}$ or $1\frac{1}{2}$ **26** $\frac{1}{4}$ **27** $\frac{3}{5}$ **28** $\frac{2}{3}$ **29** $\frac{5}{6}$ **30** $\frac{1}{2}$ **31** 1 **32** $\frac{3}{4}$

11

1 150 **2** 56 **3** 32 **4** 48 **5** 60 g **6** 25 cm **7** 1·1 kg **8** 80 km
9 3·5 m **10** 270 ml **11** 52p **12** £1·65 **13** 40p **14** 24 **15** 1·8 m **16** £25
17 80 cm **18** 72 **19** 7·5 kg **20** 76 **21** 132 **22** 45 km **23** £4·80 **24** 1·2 km

12

1 3 **2** 8 **3** 12 **4** 10 **5** 9 **6** 60 **7** 3 **8** 21 **9** 6 **10** 13 **11** 2·5 **12** 8

13

1 560 **2** 4500 **3** 1800 **4** 24 000 **5** 60 **6** 8 **7** 5 **8** 30 **9** 12 **10** 5
11 90 **12** 60 **13** 720 **14** 3500 **15** 56 000 **16** 13 200 **17** 4500 **18** 270 **19** 48 000 **20** 4800
21 700 **22** 500 **23** 30 **24** 80 **25** 12 **26** 1100 **27** 60 **28** 700 **29** 63 000 **30** 3600
31 3300 **32** 300 **33** 200 **34** 28 000 **35** 640 **36** 3600 **37** 12 **38** 90 **39** 6 **40** 70
41 8 **42** 11 **43** 40 **44** 80 **45** 42 000 **46** 12 100 **47** 1080 **48** 5400

14

1 5728 **2** 3427 **3** 30 240 **4** 14 415 **5** 15 903 **6** 42 728 **7** 128 466 **8** 105 532 **9** 196 266 **10** 146 225 **11** 86 976 **12** 192 038 **13** 257 808 **14** 112 941 **15** 214 098

15

1 0·3 **2** 1·7 **3** 0·04 **4** 0·752 **5** 1·68 **6** 0·05 **7** 5·38 **8** 0·021 **9** 0·018 **10** 0·372 **11** 4·5 **12** 0·004 **13** 1·297 **14** 0·06 **15** 0·009 **16** 0·505 **17** 900 **18** 2280 **19** 500 **20** 6 **21** 39 **22** 240 **23** 600 **24** 2 **25** 200 **26** 43 **27** 60 **28** 1009 **29** 515 **30** 8 **31** 2031 **32** 84 **33** 200 **34** 12·5 **35** 90 **36** 52·5 **37** 56 **38** 240 **39** 36 **40** 120

16

1

Length	Width	Perimeter	Area
12 cm	8 cm	40 cm	96 cm^2
9 cm	9 cm	36 cm	81 cm^2
24 cm	5 cm	58 cm	120 cm^2
11 cm	3 cm	28 cm	33 cm^2
20 cm	20 cm	80 cm	400 cm^2
17 cm	5 cm	44 cm	85 cm^2

2 *a* 3 cm *b* 8 cm Area 96 cm^2 Perimeter 42 cm
3 *c* 10 cm Area 220 cm^2 Perimeter 70 cm
4 *d* 10 cm Area 1300 cm^2 Perimeter 200 cm
5 Area 20 cm^2 Perimeter 18 cm

17

1 268 **2** 68 cm **3** 2·8 litres **4** 2·325 kg **5** 3 m 85 cm **6** 1·765 litres **7** 145 g **8** 1·218 km

18

1 80 km **2** 128 km **3** 16 km **4** 70 km **5** 96 km **6** 25 miles **7** 55 miles **8** 70 miles **9** 40 miles **10** 90 miles **11** 280 real **12** 320 real **13** 160 real **14** 70 real **15** 190 real **16** £40 **17** £86 **18** £23 **19** £60 **20** £14

19

1 A right-angled triangle
B trapezium
C irregular octagon
D irregular hexagon
E parallelogram
F regular hexagon
G isosceles triangle
H kite
I regular octagon
J scalene triangle
K kite (allow dart or quadrilateral)
L regular pentagon
M rhombus
N irregular pentagon
O regular heptagon

20

1 215 **2** 643 **3** 168 **4** 429 **5** 780 **6** 357 **7** 592 **8** 834 **9** 901 **10** 476 **11** 327 **12** 890 **13** 675 **14** 952 **15** 108 **16** 514 **17** 741 **18** 486 **19** 263 **20** 639 **21** DXLII **22** CCXXVI **23** CCCLXXXIX **24** DCIII **25** CDLXVII **26** DCCXXX **27** CLIV **28** CCXCV **29** DCCCLXXI **30** CMXVIII **31** DCLI **32** CMXXXVII **33** CCLXXXIV **34** DCCXCIII **35** DXX **36** DCCCXVI **37** CLXXIX **38** CDV **39** CMXLVIII **40** CCCLXII

21

1 562 000 562 300 600 000
2 7 235 000 7 235 100 7 200 000
3 82 000 82 000 100 000
4 9 654 000 9 654 200 9 700 000
5 2 110 000 2 109 900 2 100 000
6 4 870 000 4 870 500 4 900 000
7 5 840 740 6 000 000 5 841 000
8 2 462 900 2 000 000 2 463 000
9 617 170 1 000 000 617 000
10 1 259 650 1 000 000 1 260 000
11 6 506 380 7 000 000 6 506 000
12 8 941 530 9 000 000 8 942 000
13 4·1 4 4·06
14 13·8 14 13·79
15 2·8 3 2·83
16 298·5 298 298·49
17 0·5 1 0·55
18 20·0 20 20·00

22

1 18,36,etc **2** 21,42,etc **3** 20,40,etc **4** 33,66,etc **5** 40,80,etc **6** 52,104,etc **7** 45 **8** 20 **9** 42 **10** 60 **11** 36 **12** 66 **13** 1,3 **14** 1,3,9 **15** 1,2,3,4,6,12 **16** 1,5,25 **17** 1,2,7,14 **18** 1,2,3,6,9,18 **19** 31,37,41,43,47 **20** 71,73,79,83,89,97 **21** 111 133 333 **22** $2 \times 2 \times 7$ **23** $3 \times 3 \times 5$ **24** $2 \times 3 \times 13$
25 $2 \times 2 \times 2 \times 2 \times 2$
26 $2 \times 2 \times 5 \times 5$
27 $2 \times 3 \times 3 \times 3$

23

1 22 095 **2** 78 732 **3** 47 090 **4** 162 334 **5** 103 356 **6** 56 472 **7** 126 991 **8** 100 275 **9** 97 253 **10** 118 248 **11** 9091·6 **12** 643·34 **13** 12 070·1 **14** 1858·48 **15** 21 098·4

24

1 245 r 20 **2** 432 **3** 245 **4** 153 r 9 **5** 147 r 3 **6** 356 r 12 **7** 174 **8** 218 **9** 126 r 10 **10** 163 **11** 532 r 12 **12** 164 r 28

25

1 3 **2** 5 **3** 9 **4** 4 **5** 0 **6** 8 **7** 1·4 **8** 4·6 **9** 9·6 **10** 3·1 **11** 2·1 **12** 5·7 **13** 4·73 **14** 2·15 **15** 8·5 **16** 4 **17** 7·61 **18** 0·36 **19** 1·6 **20** 3·0 **21** 9·3 **22** 6·5 **23** 4·9 **24** 5·9 **25** 8·95 **26** 6·38 **27** 3·55 **28** 5·3 **29** 7·03 **30** 0·63 **31** 3·609 **32** 9·747 **33** 0·455 **34** 9·293 **35** 6·667 **36** 7·172

26

1 7 **2** 1600 **3** 24·5 **4** 829·4 **5** 0·06 **6** 0·8 **7** 0·303 **8** 5·297 **9** 140 **10** 0·06 **11** 390 **12** 1101 **13** 0·052 **14** 0·009 **15** 7·708 **16** 4·62 **17** 0·315 **18** 9·043 **19** 0·002 **20** 0·837 **21** 206 **22** 1509 **23** 60·5 **24** 21·2 **25** 0·4 **26** 7·91 **27** 0·48 **28** 0·036 **29** 1040 **30** 80·26 **31** 500·8 **32** 85

27

1 729·8
2 256·75
3 683·25
4 176·5
5 178·142
6 359·25
7 515·3333
8 2765·666
9 538·636
10 158·75
11 4842·5
12 712·8
13 567·25
14 862·571
15 293·833
16 437·916
17 713·777
18 468·375
19 263·5
20 159·75
21 239·6

28

1 625 m
2 435 ml
3 56 cm
4 275 g
5 1·68 m
6 2·003 kg
7 1·26 litres
8 275

29

1

Shape	Faces	Edges	Vertices
octahedron	8	12	6
hexagonal based prism	8	18	12
cuboid	6	12	8
triangular based pyramid	4	6	4
cube	6	12	8
octagonal based prism	10	24	16
pentagonal based prism	7	15	10
square based pyramid	5	8	5
triangular based prism	5	9	6

30

1 $a = 48°$
2 $b = 252°$
3 $c = 75°$
4 $d = 83°, 97°$
5 $e = 6$ cm
6 $f = 7$ cm
7 $g = 8$ cm, 6 cm
8 $h = 5$ cm
9 4 m, 7 m
10 12 m, 11 m
11 5 m, 7 m, 5 m
12 15 m, 43 m
13 30 cm, 15 cm
14 17 m, 10 m
15 $q = 20$ m
16 $5r = 22·5$ m

31

1 253
2 176
3 $249\frac{10}{35}$
4 185
5 $397\frac{1}{19}$
6 328
7 164
8 $150\frac{7}{54}$
9 3·82
10 3·79
11 19·4
12 1·36

32

1 100 698
2 6·25 litres
3 £1·35
4 25 m
5 48
6 27 000 kg
7 167 km
8 £6·95

33

1 <
2 =
3 >
4 <
5 <
6 <
7 >
8 =
9 >
10 >
11 =
12 >
13 =
14 <
15 <
16 <
17 $\frac{3}{5}$ $\frac{5}{8}$ $\frac{13}{20}$ $\frac{2}{3}$
18 $\frac{3}{8}$ $\frac{4}{10}$ $\frac{5}{12}$ $\frac{1}{2}$
19 $\frac{7}{6}$ $\frac{11}{9}$ $\frac{15}{12}$ $\frac{4}{3}$
20 $\frac{5}{4}$ $\frac{8}{6}$ $\frac{7}{5}$ $\frac{3}{2}$
21 $\frac{5}{8}$
22 $\frac{7}{20}$
23 $\frac{5}{6}$
24 $\frac{5}{24}$
25 $\frac{38}{45}$
26 $\frac{13}{21}$

34

1 $1\frac{3}{8}$
2 $1\frac{3}{12}$
3 $\frac{2}{6}$
4 $\frac{5}{10}$
5 $\frac{11}{12}$
6 $1\frac{3}{10}$
7 $\frac{23}{40}$
8 $\frac{4}{15}$
9 $7\frac{4}{10}$
10 $4\frac{2}{9}$
11 $4\frac{4}{12}$
12 $1\frac{71}{100}$
13 $3\frac{23}{30}$
14 $7\frac{13}{24}$
15 $2\frac{3}{14}$
16 $1\frac{25}{36}$
17 $1\frac{11}{20}$
18 $2\frac{5}{6}$

35

1 41%
2 10%
3 8%
4 99%
5 80%
6 1%
7 25%
8 70%
9 50%
10 58%
11 30%
12 95%
13 9%
14 75%
15 20%
16 44%
17 a) $\frac{9}{10}$ **b)** 0·9
18 a) $\frac{57}{100}$ **b)** 0·57
19 a) $\frac{1}{4}$ **b)** 0·25
20 a) $\frac{17}{25}$ **b)** 0·68
21 a) $\frac{3}{100}$ **b)** 0·03
22 a) $\frac{3}{5}$ **b)** 0·6
23 a) $\frac{7}{50}$ **b)** 0·14
24 a) $\frac{9}{20}$ **b)** 0·45
25 29
26 80
27 40p
28 1·6 cm
29 14
30 105
31 450 ml
32 1·2 litres
33 12
34 13·5
35 600 m
36 4·95 km
37 50
38 3
39 20p
40 75 g

36

1 a) 80 miles **b)** 150 miles
2 a) 125 **b)** 60
3 a) 300 g **b)** 1 kg
4 a) 240 m **b)** 2·8 km
5 a) 4 : 3 **b)** 30%
6 a) £2·25 **b)** £4·80 **c)** £2·24
7 a) 900 ml, 300 ml **b)** 2 m, 80 cm **c)** £80, £100

37

1 120 cm^3
2 162 cm^3
3 360 cm^3
4 112 cm^3
5 5000 cm^3
6 900 cm^3
7

Length	Width	Height	Volume
10 cm	6 cm	6 cm	360 cm^3
40 cm	25 cm	20 cm	20 000 cm^3
12 cm	9 cm	4 cm	432 cm^3
22 cm	14 cm	5 cm	1540 cm^3
20 cm	12 cm	12 cm	2880 cm^3
24 cm	15 cm	10 cm	3600 cm^3

8 125 cm^3
9 30 cm
10 3·5 m

38

1 214 m
2 185 ml
3 £8·60
4 675 g
5 18 minutes
6 £334·80

39

1

Colour	Customers
blue	10
grey	2
pink	4
white	24

Sport	Competitors
cycling	108
running	144
swimming	90
other	18

40

1 F
2 N
3 B
4 Y
5 L
6 U
7 H
8 T
9 (−2, −3)
10 (3, −5)
11 (−4, 4)
12 (6, 3)
13 (−4, 0)
14 (0, −4)
15 (4, −3)
16 (−5, −2)
19 parallelogram
20 square
21 (−4, 1)
22 (2, −4)
23 (−3, 0)
24 (−1, −5)

41

1 7°C
2 −7°C
3 15°C
4 −16°C
5 3°C
6 −11°C
7 10°C
8 18°C
9 9°C
10 26°C
11 19°C
12 14°C
13 5°C
14 4°C
15 31°C
16 −12°C
17 −3°C
18 −5°C
19 1°C
20 −13°C
21 8°C
22 −19°C
23 −4°C

24

Old	Change	New
2°C	−8°C	−6°C
−7°C	+12°C	5°C
−3°C	−15°C	−18°C
19°C	−23°C	−4°C
−23°C	+7°C	−16°C
−5°C	−9°C	−14°C

Old	Change	New
−3°C	+6°C	3°C
−10°C	+4°C	−6°C
8°C	−21°C	−13°C
−1°C	+5°C	4°C
−15°C	+8°C	−7°C
16°C	−17°C	−1°C

42

1 −2°C
2 −10°C
3 −7°C
4 5°C
5 −9°C
6 4°C
7 1°C
8 −1°C

9

Old	Change	New
−8°C	+5°C	−3°C
11°C	−8°C	3°C
−1°C	−3°C	−4°C
−4°C	+9°C	5°C
1°C	−7°C	−6°C
−10°C	+2°C	−8°C

10

Old	Change	New
1°C	−3°C	−2°C
−2°C	+6°C	4°C
6°C	−10°C	−4°C
5°C	−7°C	−2°C
20°C	−15°C	5°C
−6°C	+3°C	−3°C

11 −6
12 2
13 −6
14 −3
15 −13
16 −5
17 4
18 8
19 2
20 18
21 1
22 −3
23 −9
24 −15
25 3
26 5
27 11
28 13
29 −11
30 −4
31 4
32 −8
33 −8
34 −18
35 −7
36 7
37 3
38 −8
39 −25
40 18

43

1 4·8
2 2·4
3 2·7
4 7·7
5 1·2
6 0·4
7 0·5
8 1·1
9 0·9
10 0·6
11 1·2
12 0·8
13 4·2
14 8·4
15 1·6
16 7·2
17 3·6
18 5·5
19 6·3
20 14·4
21 0·5
22 0·3
23 0·7
24 0·8
25 1·1
26 0·4
27 0·8
28 1·2
29 1·5
30 5·4
31 12·1
32 2·4
33 4·0
34 4·8
35 13·2
36 3·6
37 0·7
38 1·1
39 0·5
40 0·3
41 0·9
42 0·8
43 1·2
44 0·8
45 4·5
46 4·9
47 4·4
48 7·2

44

1 13
2 25
3 33
4 45
5 17
6 18
7 58
8 53
9 16
10 26

45

1 5
2 19
3 39
4 25
5 105
6 238
7 20
8 9
9 9
10 $2 \times (3 + 4) = 14$
11 $(72 \div 12) \times 3 = 18$
12 $5 \times (7 - 3) = 20$
13 $(16 + 8) \div 2 = 12$
14 $9 \times (5 - 2) = 27$
15 $(20 \div 5) - 1 = 3$
16 $(4 + 8) \times 2 = 24$
17 $90 \div (10 + 5) = 6$
18 $(20 - 15) \div 5 = 1$
19 $2 - (0{\cdot}5 \times 3) = 0{\cdot}5$
20 $12 + (8 \div 4) = 14$
21 $(4 \times 6) + 2 = 26$

46

1 0·2
2 8·4
3 0·072
4 0·18
5 0·006
6 0·04
7 0·8
8 0·007
9 0·22
10 0·024
11 0·28
12 0·081
13 0·05
14 0·6
15 0·009
16 0·07
17 0·015
18 0·4
19 0·048
20 4·2
21 0·009
22 0·02
23 0·6
24 0·008
25 418·8
26 382·77
27 7·65
28 590·73
29 7·8
30 3·8
31 0·84
32 0·63

48

2 8·5 cm
3 3·7 cm
4 6·3 cm
5 0·65 m
6 15·6 cm
7 11 cm
8 1·48 m
9 19·8 cm

49

1 *x*1 *y*5
*x*2 *y*2
2 *x*2 *y*2
*x*6 *y*1
3 *x*1 *y*9
*x*3 *y*4
4 *x*3 *y*5
*x*7 *y*2
5 *x*2 *y*4
*x*5 *y*2
6 *x*2 *y*9
*x*5 *y*4
7 2 fours, 7 sixes
5 fours, 5 sixes
8 fours, 3 sixes
11 fours, 1 sixes
8 3 fives, 18 eights
11 fives, 13 eights
19 fives, 8 eights
27 fives, 3 eights
9 *x*1 *y*18
*x*2 *y*13
*x*3 *y*8
*x*4 *y*3
10 *x*1 *y*10
*x*3 *y*7
*x*5 *y*4
*x*7 *y*1
11 *x*2 *y*11
*x*7 *y*7
*x*12 *y*3

50

1 0·2 0·4 0·6 0·8 1·0 1·2
2 −3 −2 −1 0 1 2
3 $1\frac{1}{2}$ $1\frac{3}{4}$ 2 $2\frac{1}{4}$ $2\frac{1}{2}$ $2\frac{3}{4}$
4 $\frac{3}{8}$ $\frac{3}{4}$ $1\frac{1}{8}$ $1\frac{1}{2}$ $1\frac{7}{8}$ $2\frac{1}{4}$
5 1 0·95 0·9 0·85 0·8 0·75
6 22 41 60 79 98 117
7 1 $1\frac{2}{3}$ $2\frac{1}{3}$ 3 $3\frac{2}{3}$ $4\frac{1}{3}$
8 −12 −8 −4 0 4 8
9 100 101 102 103 104 105
10 0·01 0·02 0·03 0·04 0·05 0·06
11 3 2 1 0 −1 −2
12 0·5 3 5·5 8 10·5 13
13 −7 −5 −3 −1 1 3
14 0·3 0·6 0·9 1·2 1·5 1·8
15 2·005 2·01 2·015 2·02 2·025 2·03
16 100 175 250 325 400 475

51

1 20 cm^2
2 35 cm^2
3 96 cm^2
4 32·5 cm^2
5 27 cm^2
6 38·5 cm^2
7 15 cm^2
8 36 cm^2
9 112 cm^2
10 72 cm^2
11 105 cm^2
12 180 cm^2

52

1 553 213
2 2 043 948
3 580 615
4 2 421 685
5 5 086 232
6 226 281
7 1 286 057
8 497 888
9 445 413
10 920 064
11 213 359
12 1 708 457
13 673 913
14 370 975
15 2 097 625
16 749 478
17 2100
18 108
19 0·5
20 3·4
21 144
22 4
23 0
24 24·5
25 3200
26 0·57
27 25·2
28 108
29 12
30 0
31 40
32 10·8

53

1 11 152
2 11 307
3 34 140
4 45 333
5 28 413
6 32 599
7 33 584
8 58 380
9 34 370
10 23 556
11 41 661
12 22 064
13 44 744
14 68 950
15 116 909
16 172 584
17 60 021
18 153 630

54

1 284
2 $739\frac{2}{4}$
3 548
4 $172\frac{10}{12}$
5 $951\frac{3}{5}$
6 $467\frac{4}{8}$
7 629
8 $893\frac{1}{6}$
9 5·46
10 75·3
11 3·65
12 63·9
13 428
14 159
15 $183\frac{18}{29}$
16 $274\frac{12}{17}$
17 2·65
18 31·65

55

1 $\frac{1}{10}$
2 $\frac{1}{6}$
3 $\frac{1}{4}$
4 $\frac{2}{5}$
5 $\frac{7}{12}$
6 $\frac{1}{4}$
7 $\frac{5}{24}$
8 $\frac{8}{15}$
9 $\frac{9}{16}$
10 $\frac{1}{14}$
11 $\frac{1}{14}$
12 $\frac{1}{8}$
13 $\frac{2}{15}$
14 $\frac{1}{6}$
15 $\frac{5}{24}$
16 $\frac{1}{16}$
17 $\frac{2}{21}$
18 $\frac{1}{12}$
19 $\frac{2}{9}$
20 $\frac{3}{20}$

56

1 1 : 20
2 1 : 400 000
3 1 : 1000
4 1 : 500
5 1 : 30 000
6 1 : 10
7 1 : 2500
8 1 : 800
9 6·2 km
10 1·56 m
11 375 m
12 11·6 m
13 2·075 km
14 470 km
15 1 : 100
16 1 : 100 000
17 1 : 4000
18 1 : 5 000 000
19 1 : 250
20 1 : 20 000

57

1 9 : 30
2 12 : 30
3 3 : 30
4 20 miles
5 120 miles
6 180 miles
7 1 hour
8 30 minutes
9 1h 30 mins
10 40 miles
11 60 miles
12 20 miles

58

1 5, 320%, 64%
2 10, 35, 3·5
3 7, 112°C, 16°C
4 8, 11·6 m, 1·45 m
5 £7·50
6 7·8 cm
7 4 hours
8 6·5
9 1·8 kg
10 34

60

1 A (2, 3)(−3, −2)(2, −3)
B (−1, 4)(−4, 1)(−1, −4)
2 C (0, −2)(−2, 0)(0, 2)
D (4, −2)(−2, 4)(4, 2)
3 E (−2, −4)(4, 2)(2, −4)
F (−3, −1)(1, 3)(3, −1)
4 G (−2, 1)(1, −2)(2, 1)
H (−4, −1)(−1, −4)(4, −1)

61

1 17·4
2 £350
3 −2
4 0·015 kg
5 173 555
6 £53·10
7 79°
8 0·43
9 225 cm^2
10 4·975
11 210
12 6·143
13 4·5 cm
14 699 400
15 $\frac{7}{12}$
16 5·3 m
17 450 ml
18 50 000
19 80 cm
20 30

62

1 80 000
2 3 000 000
3 500
4 900 000
5 4000
6 $\frac{6}{100}$
7 70
8 $\frac{2}{1000}$
9 223 832
228 328
232 388
232 833
10 1 009 919
1 010 019
1 011 901
1 019 001
11 6 567 675
6 575 655
6 655 676
6 756 575
12 3 760 000
13 260 000
14 6 020 000
15 500 000
16 10·03
17 5·5
18 902·57
19 7·65
20

Old	Change	New
3°C	−5°C	−2°C
−8°C	+15°C	7°C
−4°C	−7°C	−11°C
−6°C	+10°C	4°C

Arabic	Roman
579	DLXXIX
943	CMXLIII
728	DCCXXVIII
496	CDXCVI

63

1 $6\frac{1}{4}$
2 $4\frac{3}{20}$
3 $2\frac{1}{2}$
4 $\frac{5}{6}$
5 $\frac{2}{5}$
6 $\frac{5}{14}$
7 $\frac{11}{16}$
8 $\frac{2}{9}$
9 $\frac{3}{10}$
10 $\frac{1}{8}$
11 $\frac{3}{22}$
12 $\frac{1}{15}$
13 3·6
14 0·042
15 0·24
16 0·06
17 0·09
18 0·007
19 0·009
20 0·08
21 32
22 514·6
23 0·027
24 0·68
25

Fraction	Decimal	% age
$\frac{3}{10}$	0·3	30%
$\frac{3}{4}$	0·75	75%
$\frac{7}{100}$	0·07	7%
$\frac{4}{5}$	0·8	80%

26 £280
27 150 ml
28 0·35 litres
29 15 cm
30 £19.80

64

1 16	**9** 9	**17** 56 cm^2, 34 cm
2 2·3	**10** 64	**18** 92 cm^2, 46 cm
3 0·058	**11** 1350	**19** 40 cm^2
4 1·9	**12** 20	**20** 154 cm^2
5 0·01	**13** 2700	**21** 36 cm^2
6 0·768	**14** 5	**22** 160 cm^2
7 250	**15** 56	**23** 280 cm^3
8 7·5	**16** 4	**24** 9000 cm^3

65

1 regular octagon	**5** *a* 233°
2 hexagonal based prism	**6** *b* 37°
3 parallelogram	**7** *c* 51° *d* 129°
4 square based pyramid	**8** *e* 86°